Steering by a Star

An Immigrant's Journey to Prosperity

PAUL L. CRUZ

WITH KATE HENSLER FOGARTY

ISBN (paperback): 979-8-218-37520-1
ISBN (ebook): 979-8-218-37521-8

LCCN: 2024903394

ABOUT THE COVER

The opportunity to work on the The CF-105 Arrow Interceptor was a pivotal moment in my career. The CF-105 was an advanced Mach 2 fighter jet commissioned by the Canadian government, designed to fly at an altitude of 50,000 feet. Its mission was to intercept Soviet bombers flying across the North Pole to attack Canadian and US targets.

Upon my immigration to Canada, I was hired by Lucas Rotax Ltd. in Scarborough, Ontario, to work on the CF-105's main engine control and the afterburner controls. My job was to redesign certain control valve features to match changes in the engine fuel control schedules, as the engine performance was being upgraded.

As you will read, for political reasons the CF-105 project was shelved in 1959, resulting in the discharge of thousands of seasoned engineers and technicians who had been associated with the project. Most of this talent (including myself) sought employment in the United States, essentially bringing to an end a promising Canadian aircraft industry.

However, I will always consider the CF-105 project my introduction to airplane valve design, and the one that inspired me to pursue it for the rest of my career. Its failure also caused me indirectly to move to the US, which had been my dream from a young age, and eventually found my company Valve Research and Manufacturing, which has provided for my family and me for 50 years.

Where shall we adventure, to-day that we're afloat,
Wary of the weather and steering by a star?
Shall it be to Africa, a-steering of the boat,
To Providence, or Babylon or off to Malabar?

—Pirate Story, A Child's Garden of Verses,
Robert Louis Stevenson, 1885

To my beloved wife Conchita,
who was my brave companion on this adventure for fifty years.

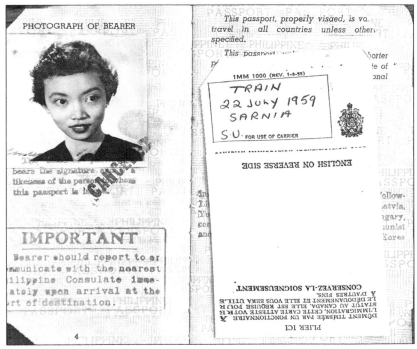

Conchita's passport from The Republic of the Philippines. She joined me in Canada in 1959, and we were married soon after.

TABLE OF CONTENTS

INTRODUCTION

For many years, when I'd tell people the story of my life they would say, "You should write a book"—as if mine was an especially fascinating story. It is true that I grew up in China, the Philippines, and Canada, came to the United States with nothing, and started my own business with very little. Now that business—designing and producing valves for the airline industry—has grown and been profitable for forty years. I had a successful and loving marriage, and today my three wonderful children work with me in the family business. But I was never convinced that my life story was something that anyone would want to read.

Perhaps I was hesitant to share my story because I come from a family in which difficult things weren't often spoken about. My father was interned for four years during World War II, and after he was released there was little discussion of his time in the internment camp, or of how my mother and their four children had survived without him. As young girls, my mother and her sister had essentially been left on the steps of an orphanage by her father after their mother died, but that wasn't a period she spoke about very often. There were hard times and tragedies in my life as well, but in my experience Asian families keep their business to themselves. To speak about such events, I felt, could bring shame on my family.

But in later years, when I began to open up and share some of my stories with friends in the United States, they were understanding rather than judgmental—even unfazed! At around the age of forty, with a comfortable job and nice home in the suburbs of upstate New York, I moved my wife and three kids to a rented apartment in Florida, having spent every penny on a failing machine shop and not realizing that the country was in a deep recession. But when I confided to a friend and fellow entrepreneur that I had taken out a second mortgage on my house, he told me, "Oh, I mortgaged my home a number of times." I realize now that everyone has challenges, and often it helps to share them with others.

I have worked nearly every day of my life for the last seventy years, and I'm very good at what I do. But when I thought about writing a book on the "secrets of my success," I had to admit that much of my success was based on luck. For example, the first big order my small business received—which allowed me to keep the doors open—was actually based on a misunderstanding! And when we moved to Florida, I had no idea that submersibles used by the oil industry would become a valuable revenue stream and for a time keep my business afloat (pardon the pun).

Another "secret of my success," I reflected, was being willing to take a risk. I changed jobs four times early in my career and moved to several cities I'd never even visited. I also relied on making cold calls for much of my career, knocking on company doors and pitching designs that I wasn't even sure I could do. When I proposed marriage via aerogram to my wife-to-be, Conchita, asking her to leave her entire family and travel on a steamship to join me in Canada, I hadn't seen her for two years. I couldn't have known just how well suited we would be for each other.

In short, I thought, who would want to read a book by someone who admits that luck and chance were as responsible for his success as talent and foresight?

I was raised in the Catholic faith and attended Catholic school for much of my life, including De La Salle University in Manila. Even as a young child I was taught that you should try to do good in the world, not just for personal gain but for the good of others as well. And over my lifetime, I myself have been the fortunate recipient of many selfless good deeds. In Shanghai during wartime, people we barely knew opened their homes and sheltered my family during air raids. Many years later when I was looking for a business to buy, a good friend who was an accountant spent his weekends helping me examine the financials of each property.

In fact, I would not have been able to finish college were it not for the kindness of others, for reasons I will explain. So when I visited De La Salle University several ago, I thought about that and decided that I wanted to provide the same opportunity for other students in need. Therefore I established the Paul L. Cruz Scholarship Grant in 2017, providing full scholarships for four mechanical engineering students each year.

It is not in my nature to boast about my success. But I did feel that I wanted these scholarship recipients, and my grandchildren and someday their grandchildren, to know a bit more about my life, and about the company that has provided for our family all these years. I realized that if I were eighteen again and a student in engineering school, I might look at an established entrepreneur like me and think, "Wow, it looks so easy."

But building my business was not easy, and it was not a flawless process. I knew everything about how to design an airplane valve but next to nothing about how to run a company. However, I am an eternal optimist. If one avenue proved to be a dead end, I went down another. I didn't ruminate over every decision. And fortunately, Conchita was an eternal optimist, too—though at certain points she had her doubts about our future, and was probably right to!

Another quality that Conchita and I shared was a spirit of adventure. As a child, I read and reread books about explorers such as Robert Scott and Roald Amundsen, who in the early twentieth century raced to reach the South Pole. In the newsreels at the movie house during wartime, I saw Japanese warplanes being manufactured and thought to myself, "When I grow up, I would like to build airplanes." When I left Manila after college to seek my fortune in Canada, I brought along a sketch of a crystal radio set, a simple radio that requires no electricity to operate. When I get there, I thought, I'll manufacture these radios and become rich!

Little did I know that, unlike back in Manila, homes in Canada had plentiful electricity, and there was already a transistor radio on every mantle. And that in America, not all the streets were paved in gold as we had believed as children—there were poor people and homeless people, just as there were back at home in Asia.

However, I did come to believe that America was the greatest country in the world, and in the end the streets *did* become paved in gold. Or rather, I paved them myself, with the help of Conchita and many others. This would not have been possible for me in the Philippines. The "American dream" is just that, and mine came true.

I have shared my life story here so that the Paul L. Cruz Scholarship Grant students at De La Salle University, along with my family and anyone else who may read it, will understand that there will be difficulties in life. You will realize that your parents have flaws, that not everyone is a good person, and that the playing field of life is not level. But if you persist, have confidence in yourself, work hard, and follow your passion, *your* American dream—like mine—can come true.

SHANGHAI

My parents were both somewhat displaced as children. Their childhood stories are difficult—and to our modern ears quite heartbreaking—but would not have been considered unusual at the time. Nor did my parents ever complain or share much of their struggle with me or my siblings. The following is what I have pieced together of their stories.

My father, Monico (Monie) Cruz, was born in Hong Kong on June 4, 1904. Hong Kong at the time was a British colony. My father was of Portuguese descent, though his parents had also been born in Hong Kong. They were a poor family. Generations before, their ancestors had emigrated from Portugal to Macau, sixty miles west of Hong Kong across the Pearl River estuary, at that time a Portuguese colony. Today a thirty-four-mile bridge and tunnel system connects Hong Kong and Macau, the longest open-sea fixed link in the world. But my ancestors likely would have traveled there by steamboat.

My cousin Francisco Cruz had a genealogical history done of our family, the details of which are recounted in his memoir, *The Eurasian Gentile* (2014). He tells how my father's parents, Henrique Jose da Cruz Sr. and Maria Conceicao Jamora, were married in a Hong Kong church on October 28, 1899. My grandfather was a widower; he had two boys and a girl from his first marriage. Of Portuguese and Filipino descent, he owned an import/export company with offices in Hong Kong and in Swatow, China.

My father's mother, Maria, is believed to have been Spanish by birth. Orphaned at an early age, she was raised by Catholic nuns in Manila. This was provided for in her parents' will, so they must have been relatively wealthy. When I was a child we called our grandmother Cha-Cha, and she was a mild-mannered, warm, religious woman. She and my grandfather had four children together: Henrique Jr, Evelyn, Monico (my father), and Roberto.

Children often don't know the hows and whys of things. But my grandparents separated or divorced, which as Catholics must have been unusual at the time. And my grandmother left Hong Kong and moved with her four young children to Shanghai in China. As a young woman, the gentle grandmother I knew clearly had a strong backbone, and nerves of steel.

Shanghai literally means "City on the Sea." It is situated on the Huangpu River where it joins up with the Yangtze River after the Yangtze's 3,900-mile journey to the Pacific. Until 1842 Shanghai was mainly a fishing village, but after the Anglo-Chinese War—also known as the First Opium War—the British named Shanghai a treaty port, opening the city to trade and industry with other countries. To give some background, by the early nineteenth century British Empire trade was heavily dependent on the importation of tea, silk, and porcelain from China, while China was *not* dependent on British exports. To counteract this imbalance, the British East India Company began to grow opium in India and allowed private British merchants to sell it to Chinese smugglers for illegal sale in China. In 1839 China attempted to seize opium stocks at the port of Canton. But the British, in the name of free trade, backed the merchants' demands. The British navy defeated the Chinese, as they had superior ships and weapons, and imposed the Treaty of Nanking—a peace treaty that ceded Hong Kong to Britain and opened trade between Britain and China.

Soon the city of Shanghai was carved up into autonomous "concessions," administered concurrently by the British, French, and Japanese, all independent of Chinese law. At the time of my childhood, the Shanghai International Settlement was composed of Americans, British, and other international residents and was home to the famous Bund waterfront area. The French concession was to the west of the old town, and the Chinese retained control over the original walled city and the area surrounding the foreign enclaves. Each colonial presence brought its own culture, architecture, and society. Many Chinese chose not to live in the walled city but in the foreign settlements, and thus began a blending of cultures and an openness to Western influence that made Shanghai unique.

Over the next few decades, Shanghai became an important industrial center and trading port, attracting 60,000 foreign businesspeople by the 1930s. With this affluence and mix of cultures, Shanghai was the place to be. It was not a city of expatriates but an alluring place where wealthy foreigners chose to move permanently, building mansions, glamorous hotels and restaurants, nightclubs, and even a racetrack. This prosperity was built, fueled, and serviced for the most part by cheap Chinese labor, as migrants came in droves from other parts of the country. Shanghai's opulence also had a dark side, as opium was still freely abused and traded, and good times often gave way to vice.

My father and his mother and siblings were leaving a difficult situation in Hong Kong in search of a better life, but Shanghai was not a welcoming place for a poor single mother of four. They struggled to survive. So at age fourteen, my father had to quit school to go to work as a clerk at Hong Kong Shanghai Banking Corporation (HSBC). HSBC was the leading foreign bank in

China through the 1920s, its office on the Bund featuring the first pair of HSBC's iconic lion sculptures guarding the steps outside. The Shanghai branch financed local tea and silk exporters and provided foreign exchange services as well as funds for Chinese traders.

My father started out at HSBC as a mail boy, delivering letters to bankers' desks and doing some clerical work. Then he advanced to doing simple accounting. He must have learned the tricks of the trade quite well, because eventually he became an accountant in his own right. My father never got a college degree and didn't even have a high school diploma. He learned what he knew the hard way, like many other young people at the time. But as I grew up, I remember his being frustrated with himself and his professional circumstances—and he was probably right to feel that way. He felt that he did all the work while his bosses with college degrees signed the documents and got all the credit. And, of course, they were paid bigger salaries. That's how the world operated in those days.

My father always told us that it was better to be the one whose money was being counted than to be the counter, and that made an impression on me.

But my father wanted something better for his children. He always imprinted this on my siblings and me: "Don't be an accountant. All you will do is count other people's money." That made an impression on me—that it was better to be the one whose money was being counted than to be the counter. I came back to those words later as I made my own career choices.

My father. 1920s or 1930s.

My mother, Madeleine Cheng, born on June 19, 1909, also had a difficult childhood. She was full-blooded Chinese, born in Canton as the third or fourth of seven or eight children. Her mother died when she was a child, and her father couldn't handle his many children. Or rather, he couldn't handle all his daughters. In China, even today, males are thought to be more important because they are in theory stronger, work and earn money, and will take care of their parents in old age. I assume my grandfather was a farmer. Sons were considered useful on the farm, but girls weren't.

My grandfather sent my mother and her younger sister to Shanghai to live with their oldest sister, Jean Valentine, whom I would come to know as my "rich auntie." Her husband was a Frenchman who became the chief of police of the French concession there. Well off because of his position, my uncle had a car and a chauffeur. He and Aunt Jean took in my mother and her sister. But they had two girls of their own, Marie-Louise and Paulette, and I assume they eventually decided that it was best to send the two sisters to a Catholic orphanage run by French nuns. This was probably a boarding school or convent, but my mother always referred to it as an "orphanage." The Western names Madeleine and Martha were most likely assigned to my mother and her sister upon arrival. Much in the way that immigrants to America adopted new names, these little girls from the countryside had to renounce their Chinese names to assimilate in this unfamiliar new environment.

But it many ways their time at the convent was fortunate. My mother and aunt learned French and English as well as Chinese. By the time my mother left the "orphanage," she had earned her high school diploma. I still have it; it is written in Chinese characters. My mother then went to night school to learn stenography and shorthand. She spoke English and worked in English-speaking offices. And she was quite modern and stylish. She became a flapper, one of many young women in the 1920s who wore skirts above their knees, bobbed their hair short, and danced at jazz clubs. Young people loved to pose for professional photos in those days. I have a treasured photo of her dressed in chic Western style, with glossy bobbed and waved hair, a form-fitting white evening dress, silk heels, elegant jewelry, and a jacket of what appears to be Mongolian lamb.

雨洋女子英專鄭美秀女士之舞姿 （金伯陶）
Miss Chen Mei-hsiu, student of Nanyang English Girl School.

My mother, "Miss Chen Mei-hsiu, student of Nanyang English Girl School," 1930s. She worked as a secretary in Shanghai before she got married, taking shorthand, typing, etc.

My mother loved to have pictures taken of her. 1920s or 1930s.

While I don't know the details of how my parents met, many young couples at the time gathered in dance halls. Shanghai was a cosmopolitan city, and elegant restaurants, cabarets, and ballrooms lined the downtown streets. In the 1920s and 1930s Shanghai was as famous as Paris, London, or New York for its nightlife, and foreigners, travelers, and young Chinese flocked to the night spots every night.

My parents in the 1930s.

My parents' wedding photo, early 1930s.
They had a large wedding.

My parents married in 1931 or 1932, and I—their first child—was born on June 24, 1934. My brother John was born in 1935, and Joseph followed in 1937. Olivia was born in 1939, so my parents had four kids in the span of five years. When my father and mother first met, my father couldn't speak either Chinese or French well. Their only common language was English, and we were raised with English as the primary language in our family. English was the language spoken at HSBC, where my father worked, and throughout the commercial world in China in those days.

Me as a baby in Shanghai. 1934 or 1935.

*With my father 1934-35,
in a park in Shanghai.*

Me as a toddler, Shanghai. mid 1930s.

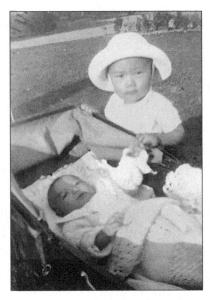

*Me with my little brother John
in Shanghai.*

For a short time we lived in a very primitive apartment, with no indoor plumbing. But then we moved to the two-story row house that I think of as my childhood home, a rented apartment just a few miles from the center of downtown Shanghai. The living quarters were on the upper floor, with an empty room on the main floor where we played ball or had fun with our dog, Nellie. Nellie was a cross between a Doberman and a police dog. My brothers and I shared the third-floor attic. There was a small servants' quarters, separated from our room by a thin wall. My mother and father and sister shared a bedroom, though it was more of an alcove off the main living space. We had running water and a flush toilet—considered quite modern in those days—but no hot water. If we wanted to take a bath, we had to heat the water on the stove and pour it into the bathtub. But that required a lot of water and time, so more often than not we just dampened a cloth in warm water and wiped ourselves clean.

Shanghai has seasons; the winters were freezing cold, and there was often snow, while the summers could be unbearably hot. The apartment had electricity but no central heating. We had a pot-bellied stove that we had to feed with wood or coal to keep ourselves warm. We had an insulated ice box but no refrigerator. The iceman would deliver brick-sized chunks of ice, which would keep food cool for several days. In the summer there was no air conditioning, so we kept the windows open. But there were no screens, so we slept under mosquito nets to protect us at night.

The global political situation at the time of my birth was tense, about to affect both my own small world and the entire planet quite dramatically. Amid the glamor and Westernization of Shanghai, the Communist Party held its first meeting in 1921 in Shanghai. By the 1930s and '40s—when I was living in Shanghai—the city had suffered raids and invasions, and the Japanese presence loomed.

Most people believe that World War II started in 1939. True, that is when Germany invaded Poland and the European war began in earnest, but the Japanese and the Germans were allies before that. Japan was somewhat like England, which had few natural resources so had looked to colonization to create the British Empire and to garner wealth and prestige. Japan also needed natural resources, but politics was not complying and they were sanctioned by various nations—so they chose to invade. They set their sights on Indonesia for oil and on China, which was larger, more populous, and richer, with natural resources than Japan.

In 1937, when I was three years old, the Japanese invaded China, basically without much resistance as the Japanese had a superior military force. It was economics plus the ambition to be a dominant nation in the region. However, the Japanese did not take over Shanghai, so everything remained quite peaceful for us. There had been some fighting and raids, but the British didn't have any troops there. My parents and many others never really believed that the Japanese troops would reach Shanghai.

However, when I ask myself what my earliest memory is, I'm taken back to the second-story balcony of our rented apartment in Shanghai. I was looking down on the street through the metal railing and suddenly saw a convoy of trucks carrying what looked like slaughtered pigs or other animals going to the marketplace. I was just looking on innocently when suddenly my mother came over and pulled me over. "Don't look at that," she said. "Go inside."

For most of my life I didn't understand that incident, though it stuck in my mind. Then several decades later. in 2019, I visited Normandy in France with my friend Fred Bauman. Fred and I are World War II buffs. In a museum there I happened to notice an item about China, and I discovered that World War II started not in Europe but in Shanghai, you might say. When the Japanese in 1937 conducted a full-scale invasion of Shanghai, Nanjing, and several other major cities, the second Sino-Japanese War began. A lot of Chinese were killed, and Japanese as well—an astounding number of people.

I discovered that when the Japanese invaded Shanghai, they bombed a very busy downtown area, killing thousands of Chinese. To get rid of the bodies, they piled them up in trucks and hauled them away. I put the pieces together and realized that was what I had seen from my balcony. So I said to myself, "Ah, I became conscious of the world in 1937, when I was three years old."

I became conscious of the world in 1937,
when I was three years old.

Things were tense but stable in Shanghai over the next few years. Adults were required to wear armbands identifying them-selves as B (British), A (American), or N (Dutch). My father, wearing his red "B" armband, continued to work. As he was born in Hong Kong, he was a British subject and had a British passport.

Two years later, in 1939, Germany invaded Poland. The US entered World War II in 1941 following the Japanese strikes on Pearl Harbor in Hawaii and on the Philippines, intended to shield Japan's drive southward to seize the oil and natural resources of Southeast Asia and the Dutch East Indies (now Indonesia) by attacking US fighter bases. The Japanese imprisoned citizens of Japanese-occupied territories—including Shanghai—in camps around Asia. This included American and British civilians and other Europeans who were not allied with Germany. The Imperial Japanese Government interned approximately 130,000 Allied civilians over the course of the war.

Allied residents of Shanghai were ordered to one of six internment camps. Sadly, this order extended to my father. My mother was Chinese, and since China was allied with Japan, she was not subject to the order. Not to mention that it would have been impossible for the Japanese to intern a Chinese population of one billion—they were happy to let them starve on their own. Food was in short supply. When they found out that my mother was Chinese and had four children, the Japanese officials were more than happy to let the responsibility of feeding and keeping them alive fall on her. If we had been British subjects, we would all have been interned.

I remember the day my father left for Pootung Civilian Assembly Center. The announcement was made that he had to report a certain area where the Japanese military put internees in boats and sent them to the internment camps. Pootung Civilian Assembly Center was on an island off the Huangpu River. If you look at photos of the Bund in Old Shanghai, along the river you can see on the opposite shore a flat piece of land where the Japanese converted warehouses into living quarters for Americans, British, and other European internees who were considered enemies of Germany or Japan. Today Pootung is a megacity with skyscrapers. No trace of the camp remains.

My father took only a suitcase to the camp. My mother accompanied him to the staging area. I was just seven years old. I could tell that my parents were upset, but because they didn't want to traumatize us kids they didn't show much of their emotions.

My mother was an amazing woman—resourceful, strong, enterprising. It was part of her heritage: the Chinese are known around the world as being very industrious. I believe I became an entrepreneur because of that gene in my mother. My father didn't have it; he was more laid back. Later my mother was the one who really encouraged us to go to college. My father would say, "Well, I went to work at the age of fourteen and did okay. So these kids should be able to do the same." But my mother would insist, "Oh, no. They are going to go to college."

I said to someone recently, "The reason I'm frugal is because of my mother." The Chinese are known for being frugal as well as hardworking. Raised during the Great Depression, most men and women were careful about money. My parents had some savings, and my mother was always in charge of the household financials. My father would earn the money and give it to her, and she would make sure that it was well spent.

My mother's Chinese heritage made her resourceful, strong, and enterprising. I believe I became an entrepreneur because of that gene.

But now it was wartime. There was little food or work. To survive this uncertain period, my mother was going to have to get creative and save her pennies in order to save our lives.

The Japanese issued coupons for rice, meats, poultry, dry goods, and other foodstuffs. This led to a secondary market of trading or selling coupons. If a pound of meat was $5 (or the equivalent in Chinese yuan), vegetarians would sell their meat coupons for whatever they could get: $1 US, or $2 US if someone could afford it. The currency in China was the yuan, but that was basically worthless; the only currencies people valued at the time were the British pound, the US dollar, or gold bars.

My mother, taken at the start of WWII (1941?).

My mother would solicit coupons from people, paying as little as she could for them. Then she would go to the store to buy goods and store them in our basement. Once she'd accumulated enough rice—which was much in demand—she would combine all of it in a great big sack and transport it to a distributor, to be sold to those who could afford it. Or she would sell to rich Shanghai individuals, who would say, "I know this was a couponed rice at one time, but I'll buy it."

In essence, my mother created a stream of business on the black market, and our ground-floor playroom became her storehouse. The Japanese didn't care about this enterprise; as they said, "Well, they're not killing each other." The police didn't care; the black market was relatively out in the open. Everyone would buy things illegally. My mother basically dealt in dry goods—beans, rice, bags of flour.

My family fared better than most during wartime. We didn't see much fighting because we were in the downtown area, which was well protected. Most of the devastation took place on the outskirts of the city, which I wouldn't witness until the war was over. Due to my mother's ingenuity and strong character, we had very little but got by, and we went to school every day "as normal." We had only the bare necessities, but we weren't starving. We ate mostly white rice and a lot of vegetables. Eggs were scarce. We would have bread but no cheese, and maybe a little margarine. If there was any meat or fish, it was mixed in with the rice and vegetables as a special treat. We never had the feeling that we were deprived.

During wartime we had very little, but we got by. We never had the feeling that we were deprived.

But that doesn't mean that we as children weren't affected by what we saw and experienced. One morning we found a straw basket with something wrapped inside. And my mother said, "That's a child." A dead baby, right by our doorstep. We were extremely upset. When the cart came around, the men simply picked up the basket and threw it in the back. This was such a common occurrence that they didn't even bother opening it up.

And we would hear all kinds of stories about people smuggling opium into the country. Opium was banned by the Japanese, but the Chinese were already so hooked on it that they would do anything to get it. Once I heard my mother talking with her friends about a woman who had a child that was stillborn. She had slit open the child's stomach and stashed opium inside to smuggle it across the border. Who knows if that was true? But hearing these stories as a kid disturbed me greatly.

Eventually we became numb; these upsetting episodes were accepted as part of wartime life. One morning there was a dead body lying across the entrance to my school. The kids just stepped over it and walked onto the campus. The disdain for the Chinese was quite normal because they were like beggars, living on the streets, and just like today, most people didn't want to deal with that. Most people look away.

The Chinese were generally impoverished. Most families, including ours, had a Chinese servant or two, usually people from the provinces who were all but homeless. You would take them in and they would clean, take care of the kids, and even cook (though our mother did most of our cooking). These women would live in a little corner somewhere; in our apartment it was next to my room. We never mistreated them, but they did not have the privilege of sitting with us and eating with us. They would eat in the kitchen after we did, whatever leftovers we couldn't finish. We paid them a small salary every month. We even maintained a servant during the war—my mother couldn't handle all four of us children while she was out trying to work and peddle her goods. But the servants were fed; they never went hungry unless we were going hungry, too.

Some of our *ahmas,* or servants, were very young, while some were very old. None of them made much of an impression on me except for my earliest one. We called her Popo Ahma—Popo both because she couldn't pronounce my name, Paul, and because *popo* is a Chinese term of endearment for one's maternal mother-in-law. After Popo Ahma left, she got married and lived on a farm and had children of her own. We were fond of her and would visit her a few times a year, the last time just before we left Shanghai.

Our relatives had different experiences than ours during wartime. My mother's younger sister, Martha, was married to a Chinese man who had a business, so they were able to survive. My "rich auntie" Jean's husband remained the French chief of police in Shanghai. The Japanese assumed that he was an ally of Japan and Germany, and he never said he wasn't. He continued to work, but if the Germans and Japanese had known that he was Gaullist, he might have been interned as well.

Hoping to avoid internment, my father's siblings went to the Portuguese consulate in Shanghai. Even though they were British citizens born in Hong Kong, they inquired whether they could claim Portuguese citizenship because of their ancestry. Portugal was not an enemy of Japan. They renounced their British citizenship and became Portuguese citizens, and they were not interned.

I often wonder why my father didn't do the same. Perhaps he was too proud to renounce his British citizenship, or he believed that the Allies would win the war. As I've said, children never know the hows and whys of things. But when I visited my cousin Paulette a few years ago, the two of us now in old age, I asked her, "Did you know that our family had tough times during the war?" And she said, "Oh, yes." Among themselves they would talk about how tough a life we had. It was common knowledge within the family that Aunt Madeleine's husband had been sent to an internment camp and she was left all alone to take care of the four kids by herself.

We would often visit our rich Auntie Jean, and she would say, "Sit down, Paul. You're going to have to have your breakfast by yourself today because I already had mine." She would serve me poached eggs and butter and bread and bacon, to fortify me until my next visit.

The British government sent money through the Swiss Consulate to women like my mother whose husbands were imprisoned in war camps or internment camps. The Swiss government was neutral, so the Japanese allowed them to distribute the funds. They also provided our family with dental and hospital care. But it wasn't steady income; it came sporadically. And toward the end of the war the British were running out of money themselves, so they didn't give much to the Swiss. Even though the Allies had won the war in Europe in 1944, it was a period of reconstruction. The war in Asia didn't end until

August 1945, when the atomic bomb was dropped by the US in Japan and ended the Japanese occupation of Asia.

It was sometimes through the kindness of our neighbors and friends that we were able to persevere during the war. An Orthodox Jewish couple who had fled Germany lived across the street from us, and we had gotten to know them quite well. Once in a while my mother would go to their apartment to help with certain tasks not allowed for Jews on the Sabbath, like turning on a light switch. We were friendly. Toward the end of the war, my mother was having trouble trying to make ends meet, and she asked the couple if they could loan us some money. After my father was released from the internment camp and began to work again, my mother paid them back. It was a happy day.

It was sometimes through the kindness of our neighbors and friends that we were able to persevere during the war.

There were many "White Russians" in Shanghai as well, people who had fled persecution after communism took over Russia in 1917. White Russians supported the tsar; and the Jews, regardless of who controlled Russia, had always been persecuted. One of our neighbors was a White Russian named Mr. Jurovich. He was an enterprising baker who also sold all sorts of goods that seemed like luxuries to us, like candies and other treats we couldn't afford. Most of his clients were Europeans.

There were often air raids over Shanghai during the war, usually when American or British planes flew over and bombed munition factories in the outlying areas. Every time the air raid siren would go off, Mr. Jurovich would say, "Come on over and stay in the basement of my store." He would even joke, "If we ever get bombed, we've got lots of food." He had lots of delicious things in his basement. "You'll never get hungry."

I learned to swim during my father's internment. I'm not sure if that's what my mother intended when she brought us to the park one day, but that's what happened! We would often go to Shanghai's public parks on the weekend, and some of them had swimming pools. The first time we went to a park with a pool, I saw people just jumping in, so I said to myself, I'm going to do the same. The next thing I remember is a man grabbing hold of me and hoisting me out. My mother must have come screaming, "He doesn't know how to swim!" I wasn't coughing up water, so I must have held my breath. Thankfully we were at the shallow end. What I do remember very clearly is that the man was Japanese—in theory, the enemy. He was nice, and I recall being surprised that this "enemy" wasn't such a bad guy. Afterward we would come to the pool quite often; it was inexpensive, clean, and fun, and a great way for my mother to tire out her four children.

While my father was interned at Pootung, probably around 1943, my sister developed a serious case of pneumonia and had to be confined to Shanghai General Hospital. The hospital was founded by Christian missionaries in the 1800s, and during the war it was used by the Japanese army to house sick foreign prisoners. My father was informed of my sister's illness. Now it seems hard to believe, but accompanied by a Japanese soldier and an interpreter, he was able to visit my sister at the hospital.

Even more unbelievable to us as kids was the sack of chocolate bars my father brought with him! I distinctly remember the brand name: Neilson. He told my sister to give them to my mother to distribute among us. It was like manna from heaven. During the war we had hardly any chocolate, other than a small piece occasionally at my rich aunt's home. It seems so humane on the part of the Japanese to allow my father to visit his gravely sick daughter—with chocolates? He must have brought a dozen thick bars, dark and milk chocolate. I learned that Neilson was a Canadian company that made chocolate for the Canadian troops and the Canadian Red Cross. The chocolates may have been distributed to the Pootung internees through the Swiss Red Cross, and perhaps my father's friends had all gifted him their rations.

My mother and father were reunited at the hospital. The "interpreter" was actually a family friend who'd been interned along with my father—of Portuguese descent but British, just like him. He had done a lot of import-export business with the Japanese and could speak the language, so perhaps he acted as an unofficial interpreter in the camp.

The Japanese security officer allowed the interpreter and my father to be on leave, you might say, for the whole day. My father came back to the house for the afternoon; then the interpreter picked him up and they headed back to the camp. I wish I could find out more about the Japanese commandant of Pootung, because it seems like internment at that camp was, while difficult, less brutal than at other camps. There is no question that the Japanese were unspeakably vicious foes during World War II: the stories of how ruthlessly they treated prisoners of war, citizens, women, children are countless. Even today there is talk of restitution. But at Pootung, the internees were able to create gardens, have sporting teams, ply their sewing and other trades, perform plays and operas. It's a little-known fact of the war, and I think it's important to mention.

Having been raised in a convent, my mother was Catholic. Her parents were probably Buddhists, but when we were growing up she considered herself a Catholic. My father, being of Portuguese descent, was also Catholic, but he was not especially religious. We did go to church every Sunday, and my mother had a statue of Christ that she would say a prayer in front of every morning, and maybe light a candle. My brother and I received our First Communions when we were seven or eight, during my father's internment. Afterward we had a small celebration and a few cookies at our home, with mainly relatives in attendance.

First Communion Party, Shanghai, 1942.
My brother John (at left) and me in white suits. My father
was interned in a World War II internment camp. We were given
watches as a gift by our family friend Uncle Madsen.

Also attending was one of my father's friends, whom we knew as Uncle Matsen. He was Danish and therefore not interned. (I don't know his first name, because we were taught to address our parents' friends as "Uncle" or "Auntie.") Uncle Matsen was married to a beautiful Japanese woman, and they didn't have any children. At one time they lived upstairs in our home.

While my father was interned Uncle Matsen would often visit us, bringing cookies and cakes, or invite us to dinner. At our First Communion party, he surprised my brother and me with our first wristwatches. It was a kind thing to do, and I treasured mine.

A few years later, when our family was preparing to move to the Philippines, we couldn't bring our dog Nellie on the steamship. Uncle Matsen said, "I'll take care of Nellie for you." (I don't know if that actually happened, but we children were happy to hear it at the time.) The Matsens stayed in Shanghai and then were stuck there when the communists took over. Eventually he was able to move to Hong Kong. We lost contact.

Ten years later, in 1957, my father was walking through Balagtas Apartments, our housing complex in Manila, when suddenly he saw Uncle Matsen. "What are you doing here!" he said. Uncle Madsen had moved to Manila; his wife had left him, and he was now with another Japanese woman, whom my parents met. In a time before cell phones and email, it was difficult to stay in touch with people, so this was a joyous reunion. In Shanghai and even in the Philippines, Westerners would often cluster together in certain neighborhoods, and that is most likely why the Matsens had chosen ours when they moved to Manila. My parents were also reunited with the baker, Mr. Jurovich, who had sheltered us during air raids in Shanghai. He and his family had moved to our housing complex as well. We were all neighbors again.

I also remember another "uncle" from our time in Shanghai, Uncle Sena. He wasn't a relative, just a good family friend whose visits livened up our household. An energetic person with a big personality, he was Portuguese, so he hadn't been interned. Uncle Sena had a gift for languages. He had learned Japanese, so when the Japanese were in control in Shanghai he was able to strike up a great trading business with them. The Japanese needed certain raw materials for war supplies, like iron and copper, and saw him as a local connection. Uncle would approach the officials and ask, "What do you need?" If they said, for example, "metal for bearings," he would find a supplier who mined the material and broker the deal. He made a lot of money from these connections.

Uncle Sena was fun to have around, but he had problems with drinking and gambling. I remember many times he would come over driving a brand-new car, and we would all pile in excitedly. We were so little: the four kids could all squeeze onto the back seat, my mother on the rumble seat. My father would sit in the front seat next to my uncle, and we would drive all over town. But then two weeks later he would come to our house in rags. My mother would ask, "What's happened to you?" My uncle would say, "Well, I had to pawn my suit and sell my car because I lost a lot of money at the racetrack."

Then my mother would take him in, and he'd stay at our house for a few days while he brokered a few more deals. And two weeks later he'd come with another shiny new car. I said to myself, "I'd like to be like him one day!" I was too young to recognize that Uncle Sena's habits were unhealthy. Even today I love to gamble, but I am very disciplined with myself. I like leaving the casino in the car and suit I arrived in!

> *Even today I love to gamble, but I am very disciplined*
> *with myself. I like leaving the casino in the car*
> *and suit I arrived in!*

During wartime my siblings and I tried to carry on with life as normal. As children, we were generally concerned with our own daily lives and routines. My brothers and I attended Saint Francis Xavier, an all-boys Catholic elementary school in Shanghai. My sister was just two years old at the time of my father's internment, and she stayed home with the *ahma*.

After breakfast, we walked to school. It was pleasant on warm days, but in winter it was bitterly cold and we'd bundle up. We had no uniforms. For lunch we brought wrapped sandwiches. St. Francis Xavier was an English-speaking school, with studies conducted in English. At precisely 9am the dean would blow his whistle and we'd file into school. The first subject every morning and the last one every afternoon was religion. In between we studied the usual things—English, arithmetic. I wasn't an especially devoted or good student. I ran on the track team, and the school had a small field where we would kick a soccer ball around.

After school we'd walk home to do our homework and help our mother with chores. Most of my friends at the time were neighborhood kids; my school friends lived too far away. We'd kick a soccer ball on the streets or in an open field. Marbles was our favorite activity—we played marbles all the time, and we'd try to get as many good ones as we could.

As I remember, my siblings and I got along well. With my father's absence we certainly didn't want to give our mother more stress by arguing or causing trouble. But we didn't have as much recreation as most kids do today, and we didn't have many toys. The toys that we did have were mainly hand-me-downs, but good ones, as my French uncle had a lot of rich friends who gave his children toys as gifts, and they'd give them to us when they were done with them. They weren't brand-new but were meant to last, unlike toys today. Everything now is plastic, but these were trucks and cranes made of sheet metal.

I was quite handy with tools—not to the point where I would be considered a craftsman, but I was very interested in mechanical devices. I had a chisel and a hammer, and I'd find a piece of wood and carve something out of it. I built a boat out of wood and attached a sail. I even made a submarine that was run by a rubber band turning the shaft of a propeller; it wasn't great, but it worked. And it kept me busy. My mother did find time to take us by bus to Shanghai's public gardens, often Jessfield Park. We would also go to a park close by, taking the dog along. I would sail my toy sailboat on a pond there.

I believe this interest in the mechanics of things may have helped me find and succeed in my eventual career as an engineer, as did the fact that I was ambidextrous. This skill wasn't natural but was forced upon me by my mother. Whether it was because of her Chinese upbringing or Catholic convent education, or both, she believed that to be left-handed was impolite, unfavorable, even bad luck. So when I was a young boy she insisted that I, left-handed, begin to use my right hand to eat and to write. I was hopeless at using chopsticks with my right hand, and frustrated and hungry, so we compromised. I could eat with my left hand but had to write with my right, which I eventually mastered. I still consider myself left-handed, and I played sports left-handed and left-footed. When it came to working as a design engineer later in life, I bought a left-handed drafting machine. I could do all the positioning on the scale with my left hand and was free to letter with my right, which was very beneficial.

*I was fascinated by newsreels that showed
the Japanese aircraft industry building military aircraft.
I remember thinking that building airplanes was something
I'd like to be involved with when I grew up.*

I was always interested in world events and history. We got the daily newspaper, and I enjoyed reading it and keeping track of current events. Even during the war years, the English-language newspaper was still being published. We had a radio, but during the war it was Japanese-run. We'd go to the movies occasionally, and before the main feature there would be a news-reel—also Japanese-produced. Though it was all propaganda, I was fascinated by newsreels that showed the Japanese aircraft industry building military aircraft. I remember thinking that building airplanes was something I'd like to be involved with when I grew up.

My father was interned for four years. That was a long time for a child, and a long time for an adult. During his internment we took a sampan—a flat-bottomed wooden boat—across the Whangpoo River to visit him. On Pootung there was basically nothing in those days except for a sailors' cemetery. Sailors from all over the world who died at sea or in Shanghai would be buried in this cemetery rather than being transported back to their native land—too expensive. Across from the cemetery the Japanese built the internment camp, and everything else was wild countryside.

We saw my father just three times during his internment. The first time we went to visit, the Japanese soldiers wouldn't let us get close to him. We were maybe twelve feet apart, with a fence separating us. We had to shout at each other. It was frustrating, but the Japanese were being overly cautious. The next time the Japanese allowed us to come closer. On the third visit, we met with my father in a visiting area inside the compound. The internees had built a lot of gardens and interesting areas where you could sit and talk. At first Pootung was only a men's internment camp, but in the middle of the war wives and children were allowed to be with their husbands instead of being held at a separate internment camp, which had seemed overly cruel. My father wore a red armband with his prisoner number, P-135.

Families of internees were allowed to send food parcels, so every month my mother sent extra food to the camp by post. Many of my father's friends who didn't have wives on the outside didn't have much, so he would share his food with them. One of them was a Canadian internee named Donald Crane. He was very appreciative of my father's saving his life, so to speak, as many prisoners struggled to survive or actually died from starvation. Even my father lost a lot of weight. When the war was over, Donald Crane came to live in our house. Since my mother no longer needed the downstairs as a storeroom, he and his girlfriend created some partitions and lived there until we left for Manila.

I was eleven years old when the war ended in 1945. Shanghai broke out in celebrations. There were parades downtown; we could see the fireworks from our apartment a few miles away. We saw huge crowds, partying, dancing, music. I got separated from my family in the crowds, and while it didn't seem like a big deal to me, my mother was very concerned. Everyone retraced their steps until they found me in a store, unaware that I was lost. I remember my mother being very upset, and relieved when she found me.

When the war ended and my father was released, he had a temporary job at the British consulate for a few months. Then he joined Everett Steamship Company as an accountant, and our lives seemed to take a turn for the better. We even got a home telephone—rare at the time—probably through the steamship company. Everett was founded in Shanghai in 1917 by an American who had been in the US Armed Forces. The company began as a shipping agent but moved its offices to Manila as it opened new branch offices in other Asian ports, and it started operating its own ships and managing others. During World War II, Everett lost all its ships to enemy action. But the office promptly reopened after the war and began to purchase vessels and reestablish itself. Its postwar business was built on "Liberty ships"—cargo ships that had been built in the United States to transport war materials around the world. Once the war was over, these ships were left in China. They were sold to private companies and repurposed as freighters.

Now feeling more comfortable financially, my father transferred my brothers and me to Shanghai British School, which was more expensive and elite than Xavier. For the first time I went to school with both girls and boys. Like many boys, I wasn't crazy about school but was more interested in sports. My main interest was in track and field, though I was mediocre. I liked learning cricket at the British School; it was an interesting game.

Like many boys, my brothers and I weren't crazy about school but were more interested in sports.

I was an obedient child, and I didn't have many problems with my parents. In those days, if you misbehaved it was likely that you would get a spanking. My mother did all the discipline. She'd run after me with a wooden hairbrush and threaten to hit me (though she never did). That was enough to scare me to death.

At the British School I got into a rare bit of trouble. We rode to and from school not in a yellow school bus, but in a converted US Army truck that had a canvas top and railings so that we couldn't fall out. It wasn't easy for the driver to maintain discipline in a truck like that. One day I got into a fight with another kid; I don't even remember what it was about. The bus driver reported the incident to Mr. Crow, the headmaster. We were sent to Mr. Crow's office and quickly confessed to the crime. So he said, "You're going to be caned." We both bent over, and he gave me three whacks on the behind with a rattan stick. It hurt a bit, but not enough to make me cry. It was just humiliating. Mr. Crow caned the other boy, and then we had to shake hands with each other. We shook hands with the principal, and that was it. "If you do it again," he said, "you're going to be here again tomorrow." It was all a big secret; my mother never knew about it, nor did anyone else in the family besides my brother, who'd been on the same bus. Even our classmates didn't know we'd been punished. But that was the end of my bullying days. And the other boy and I became friends afterward.

I don't remember much about holidays or vacations. I do remember riding with my family in an open truck one weekend after the war to visit Sheshan Basilica, a monumental church built by the Jesuits on a peak west of Shanghai.

But we took more excursions as a family—to the public swimming pool at Bubbling Well Road, for example. My father frequented the racetrack, though that wasn't a place for kids. The males in the family would also go to the popular YMCA on the busy Nanjing Road strip, where we were members for a while. At the Y, which was only for men, one tradition was that members swam in the indoor pool in the nude. I wasn't too crazy about the idea, but my father said, "That's okay, everyone does it." So I did it, but I was never comfortable—and the water was freezing.

After two years in Everett Steamship's Shanghai office, in 1948 my father received a permanent transfer to the head office in Manila. The job transfer was timely, because the communists in China were gaining strength. Despite the end of World War II, a civil war had continued between the nationalists and communists for control of China. The Russians were supporting the communists, and they were more organized—not to mention that Chinese nationalist leader Chiang Kai-shek was corrupt. Most of the money that the US gave Chiang Kai-shek for defense was squandered by government officials, and as a result their army was not well equipped.

The writing was on the wall that Shanghai would likely be overtaken. And quite soon after we left, that is exactly what happened, in 1949. When the communists took over China in 1949, few Western nations wanted to continue to trade with them, so the commerce that Shanghai was famous for soon collapsed. European and American banks left the country. Everett's Shanghai office shut down after a time.

Aunt Jean and her family stayed in China for five more years. Once the communists took over Shanghai, including the French sector, they were forced to leave and moved to France. My cousin Paulette was married to a Frenchman, so she went back to France with her parents. Mary-Louise's husband, Bill Orchard, worked for American Express; their office remained open after the communist takeover, so they couldn't leave. But when the economic situation didn't improve, American Express pulled out of China altogether and the family moved to New York City. They had to leave nearly everything behind. As for my father's relatives, they returned to Macau in 1951, as refugees fleeing this new totalitarian regime. They would eventually relocate to Hong Kong, which was more prosperous.

I had mixed feelings about leaving Shanghai. I had had a wonderful two years at the British School. I enjoyed it much more than Saint Francis Xavier, which had been run by strict Catholic brothers. I was sad to leave. I was beginning to learn the Queen's English, or the King's English at that time. When I left Shanghai and went to the Philippines, everyone was amazed at my British accent. And—I had discovered girls!

I remember having crushes on two girls in my class at the British School. One was Irene Dow, who sat at the desk next to me. She had been interned with her parents in the camp, as her mother was Russian and Russia was one of the Allied forces at the time. Now it seems strange that we never discussed her internment, but perhaps Irene was as boy-crazy as I was girl-crazy!

My other crush was a girl named Margaret Horidge, who sat in the first row at the desk right in front of me. It was puppy love; we never even kissed or held hands. Margaret was from Australia and had also been interned with her family, as Australia was a member of the British Commonwealth. Before I left for Manila, on my last day of school, Margaret gave me a little brass ring to remember her by. I took the ring and stuck it on my finger, but I felt kind of funny about it. I didn't want my mother to see it. When we boarded the freighter, waiting to pull anchor, I quietly dropped the brass ring into the Huangpu River. It was mainly a symbolic gesture. I didn't have a romantic attachment to Margaret. (I actually liked Irene better!) I thought, "I'm off to have a new life, full of new experiences and new romances. Why even bother thinking about it?"

I looked at the move as an adventure. We didn't have many books as children, but one that I remember well from my years in Shanghai was *A Child's Garden of Verses* by Robert Louis Stevenson. It seemed written just for me, a child cooped up in a small, crowded apartment, whose mind was just awakening to the world beyond:

> *Where shall we adventure, to-day that we're afloat,*
>   *Wary of the weather and steering by a star?*
>   *Shall it be to Africa, a-steering of the boat,*
>   *To Providence, or Babylon, or off to Malabar?*

That book got me thinking about traveling around the world and visiting all the exotic places described by Stevenson. I would read it over and over again. It was one of the reasons I was so happy to leave China for the Philippines in 1947; I saw this as the first leg of my adventure across the world. In fact, when I became a father, I bought a copy of *A Child's Garden of Verses* for my daughter. I even visited Robert Louis Stevenson's home in Edinburgh many years later.

I was happy to leave China for the Philippines; I saw this as the first leg of my adventure across the world.

As I got a little older, I became fascinated with stories of real-life explorers. I treasured a book about the race to the South Pole between Robert Scott from England and Roald Amundsen from Norway. Amundsen won the race and returned safely. Scott reached the South Pole but tragically died during his return trip, just eleven miles from his next cache of supplies. Another book I loved was about American naval officer and explorer Richard Byrd, who claimed to be the first to reach both the North Pole and the South Pole by air. These exciting adventures had occurred in the early twentieth century, which I considered relatively recent. There were many other explorers whom I admired as well and wanted to emulate when I grew up.

I wish I still had these books, but when my parents packed up our belongings to be placed in a shipping container bound for Manila, children's books didn't make the inventory list. However, two important items I stashed in my luggage did. One was a sketchbook of drawings that I'd made over the previous four years. When I was at home after school, I would draw picture after picture of imaginary boats, mainly battleships. The other was just a single page of a book. One of my American friends at the British School was a Boy Scout, and he had begun to build a crystal radio set. At the time, television hadn't been invented but everyone had a radio. And people who didn't have electricity had a crystal radio, a rudimentary radio made of inexpensive parts that used only the power of the received radio signal to produce sound. The sound was so weak that it could only be heard through earphones. I had never actually seen a crystal radio set, just the picture in the Boy Scout manual, but I was fascinated by the idea. I took the page from my friend's book and stashed it in my bag to the Philippines, with the idea that I would build one.

One of my fondest childhood memories was of the week or so before my father left on a steamship for the Philippines. We had to vacate our rented Shanghai home, so Everett put us up at the luxurious Palace Hotel on Nanjing Road. The meals were served with tablecloths, silverware, cloth napkins—all very posh and European. The setting of Western glamor and elegance, bustling with businessmen, travelers, and foreigners, seemed the perfect sendoff for the life of great adventure that awaited me.

MANILA

Preparing for the move to Manila was exciting. My father left about two months before my mother, my siblings, and I joined him. The big wooden moving crate that Everett Steamship had provided was the size of a small room, into which we packed our belongings: tables, mattresses, kitchen supplies, clothing. I remember that when the crate was delivered to our new home in the Philippines, we emptied it and then put it in the garage. We took the crate apart over time, plank by plank, to build things or give to people.

In those days no one owned their homes in Shanghai but rented—for years, decades, or even a lifetime. Housing was valuable and hard to find, so prospective renters would essentially bribe the current renters with offers of "key money" to take over their lease. If the property owner continued to get his rent, he was happy. My parents showed our apartment to several people. When they decided on one, the new renter gave them twelve gold bars, each probably about ten ounces, as key money. I had never before seen a single gold bar, let alone twelve. An ocean crossing to a far-off land with gold bars hidden in our luggage—this was shaping up to be a real adventure!

An ocean crossing to a far-off land with gold bars hidden in our luggage—this was shaping up to be a real adventure!

The move to Manila was my first trip abroad, the first time I had even been on a boat apart from traveling by sampan to visit my father at the Pootung internment camp. We would be sailing on a freighter, the cheapest means of ocean crossing.

There were passenger cruise ships and airplanes, but those were only for the rich.

As my father worked for Everett, he knew that the ships with the best passenger service were European. We took a Norwegian freighter, and it was quite a sight. Today containers are piled up on the deck of a ship, but in those days most cargo was stored in the ship's hold. Massive covers on the decks were removed, and cranes picked up the cargo and dropped it into the cavernous holds. Workers in the hold organized the items until it was filled. Then the covers were reinstalled over the hold and the deck was clear until the ship arrived at its destination.

Most freighters could accommodate only twelve paying passengers, as any more than that would require, by maritime law, that a medical doctor be on board. We had cabins on the upper deck, along with the captain and officers, and we ate with the officers in a nice dining room. The crew, on the other hand, ate wherever they could find a place to sit and slept in cramped barracks below deck. Most were sailors from Asia or Norway.

The passage took three or four days. We arrived in the Philippines in 1947, at a momentous time in the country's history. World War II had ended just a few years before, and the country was recognized by the US as a fully independent nation on July 4, 1946. The Philippines had become self-governing in 1935, but their full independence had been delayed by the war and the crippling Japanese occupation.

Portuguese explorer Ferdinand Magellan had first landed in the Philippines in 1521. The country was named for King Philip II of Spain, who was in power when it became a Spanish colony. In the late 1800s Filipinos began fighting for independence from Spain. After Spain lost to the United States in the Spanish-American War of 1898, the Treaty of Paris decreed that the US take control of the Philippines. The Filipinos fought for their independence in the brutal three-year Filipino-American War but lost. Over the next few decades, American occupation in the Philippines moved from martial law to government with some Filipino representation, accompanied by educational reform, public works, tax programs, government structure, and capital investment. Filipino "resident commissioners" were sent to the US Congress.

As I saw it, some good did come of the US occupation—compulsory education, for example. Whereas only wealthy children in the Philippines had previously gotten an education, now every Filipino child went to school and learned to read and write. The people became more educated and therefore more prosperous, and many moved to the cities.

Until World War II the Philippines continued to be governed by a semi-independent government, while the US maintained important military bases there. For that reason, on December 8, 1941—nine hours after the attack on Pearl Harbor—Japan attacked the Philippines. US forces moved to the Bataan Peninsula from Manila, hoping to save the city from destruction, but after three months of brutal combat, the combined American-Filipino army was defeated in the Battle of Bataan and the Battle of Corregidor. As in Shanghai, the Americans and their allies were interned, but guerilla resistance against the Japanese continued.

Four years of Japanese occupation decimated the country. By the time the Philippines was fully liberated by US forces in 1944, nearly one million civilians had been killed; even more were raped and pillaged. The country had suffered grave physical destruction. You may be surprised to learn that Manila was second only to Warsaw as the most devastated city in World War II.

The Republic of the Philippines was proclaimed in 1946, with a government patterned on that of the United States. But the country was still deeply dependent on the US for aid. The US was responsible for most of the redevelopment of the country—which was still very much in its early recovery stages when our family arrived in Manila Harbor. As our boat was lowered in the docks, we saw shell holes all over the seawalls. My mother said, "Oh, God, this doesn't look very good." There were bulldozers everywhere, with schools, businesses, and homes being rebuilt, but much of the city was still in rubble.

My father had found us a rental home on Balagtas Street in Pasay City, a suburb of Manila. This was one of the newly constructed townhouses built to appeal to foreigners moving to the Philippines for business. Rents were a bit more expensive than elsewhere in the city. Most of our neighbors were American or British, or other expatriates. Our house had a two-car garage on the ground level. The second level was a living and kitchen area, while the third level had two bedrooms and a small bathroom. My mother and dad and my sister slept in the master bedroom, while my brothers and I were in the other.

This photo was most likely taken just after we arrived in the Philippines in 1947. I am rear center.

We noticed the change in weather right away. As the Philippines is near the equator, the weather was hot and humid year-round—as opposed to Shanghai, which had seasons. The school year in the Philippines (June to March) was tied to the rainy and dry seasons. The climate was tropical and sticky. No one could afford air conditioning, so you had to keep your windows open to let the breeze circulate. If you were rich you might have screens on your windows and doors, but our family was at the mercy of the mosquitoes. We had a *lavandera,* a servant for washing clothes and ironing. Her residence was a small partitioned space at the end of the two-car garage. My mother cooked all the meals.

At the end of the war, the American military had abandoned a lot of its surplus war equipment in the Philippines, including ships, trucks, and in particular Jeeps. You could buy them for practically nothing. Some enterprising Filipinos bought up these Jeeps, installed roofs and seats in the back, and ferried passengers around the city. "Jeepneys" became a ubiquitous mode of public transportation; the streets were filled with these colorful, crowded makeshift buses. A ride was cheap—twenty centavos (worth a fraction of a US dollar). I would take one to school when I was running late.

My father bought himself a used Jeep and later traded it in for a used 1944 Ford convertible. In those days there were only a few types of cars: Chryslers, Fords, General Motors, Chevrolets, and Studebakers. I knew the names of every model; each had its own distinctive design. Our Ford had white-rimmed tires, which got dirty easily, so once I learned to drive I would wash them often to keep them looking halfway decent. My father took the car to work, so the rest of us walked or used Jeepneys to get around.

I began high school at De La Salle. This was an all-boys Catholic school run by the De La Salle Brothers, also known as the Christian Brothers. With a primary school, high school, and commercial secondary school, De La Salle was considered one of the better schools in Manila. World War II had been a dark time in De La Salle's history, and when I arrived the community was still recovering. The Japanese had forcibly taken over the campus and made it their South Manila headquarters. The area had been heavily bombed, with the gymnasium and much of the library destroyed. Even more tragically, in February 1945 as American forces made their way to Manila, a Japanese officer and twenty soldiers massacred all but one of the seventeen resident brothers as well as several families that had taken shelter in the school chapel. Their bodies were found by American and Filipino forces a few days later.

After the war the school was run mainly by American brothers who had been imprisoned in a Philippine internment camp during the war, along with Filipino lay teachers. They bravely resumed classes in 1945 despite the massacre and challenging conditions. As a result of the postwar focus on education, De La Salle established an undergraduate engineering school in 1947 and in later decades would expand into a university. It began accepting female students in 1973.

My alma mater, De La Salle College, Manila.
Probably 1959?

But at the time I went to De La Salle, it was still a small, single-sex school on Taft Avenue (many streets in Manila were named after American presidents). The school day started around 8 am and ended around 4 pm. I would either bring lunch or go home to eat, as I lived close by. I was not a particularly good student. I liked history, but not the way it was taught—memorization and dates, very boring. But I enjoyed learning about the history of discovery, about Christopher Columbus and other explorers.

I was a somewhat serious kid—studious, but only in subjects that interested me: science, math, and history, in particular ancient Greek and Roman history and European history relating to the rise of colonial empires. Everything else seemed like drudgery. My parents were not happy when they saw straight Ds and Cs, or even an occasional F.

> *I was a somewhat serious kid—studious, but only in the subjects that interested me: science, math, and history. Everything else was drudgery.*

I suppose I had some trouble assimilating to the American education system after being in the British system in Shanghai. The British system had been more regimented. In the American system there was more freedom. Teachers gave you the facts, but they also expected you to interject your own opinions; it was a more democratic system. The teachers wanted more participation, and I was not used to that. Also, my class in the Philippines was much larger than it had been in Shanghai, and there was no teacher's aide. You had to motivate yourself and study on your own, and I had some difficulty with that. Also, I was behind in math due to differences in the two systems. I had to take summer classes to catch up.

At De La Salle, students had to choose Spanish or Filipino as a foreign language. In Shanghai I had taken Chinese, since my mother was Chinese. Here I chose Filipino. We had to study an epic poem called *Florante at Laura*. Written in Tagalog by Filipino poet Francisco Balagtas in 1838, it is considered a masterpiece of Philippine literature. But even the Filipino students said, "This language is so antiquated, we can't understand it." And they expected *me* to understand it? Even the Filipinos would just memorize it. Most of them spoke either Tagalog (the prevailing dialect) or one of eight local dialects. The teacher knew that I was terribly behind since I had just moved to Manila, so he gave me a D so that I could pass. Most of the time I didn't even know what I was reading.

Spanish was spoken more from a cultural standpoint. Most people spoke it because it was considered more upper-class—more highfalutin, you might say. There was a certain amount of class consciousness in the language you spoke. The working class would speak Tagalog among themselves. English was the official language of communication in business, religion, and government.

High school seemed uneventful, other than sports. I had been on the track team at the British School in Shanghai, so I decided to try out at De La Salle. It turned out that I was quite fast. I ran the 400 and 800 meters; the school provided me with track spikes. I was also on the swim team but didn't enjoy that as much as track.

*We often used the swimming pool
at the Manila Hotel. 1950s.*

I became keenly interested in politics in high school. My family subscribed to a weekly international edition of *The New York Times,* which kept me informed on world news. I would also read the Philippine newspaper and listen to local politics on the radio. But I couldn't vote in the Philippines, as I wasn't a citizen.

Another complication of not being a Philippine citizen was needing to acquire a work visa, just as in the United States. My father entered the country on an H-2 visa, which allowed him to work on a temporary basis. But once he became a permanent resident, he had to leave the country and then come back in again—one of those legal formalities. So our whole family went to Hong Kong, where my father had been born. I was thrilled, because I loved to travel. Another exploration under my belt!

After a few weeks in Hong Kong, my father returned to Manila to work, but my mother and us kids stayed for more than a month longer. It was the only "family vacation" I remember. We stayed in a hotel. One day, my dad said, "We're going to visit my stepbrothers and stepsisters." I was confused, as I hadn't known until then that my grandfather had been married before he married my grandmother. Well, it turned out I had step-uncles and step-aunts, at least four of them. Between his children with his first wife and those with my father's mother, my grandfather had at least eight children.

It must have been difficult for my grandmother to move to Shanghai on her own, a single parent though not divorced—divorces weren't recognized in China at that time. But I never remember her speaking about her hardships, or my asking her about it. Difficult things were rarely spoken about in our family.

Most of my school friends in Manila were Filipino, but their heritage was a melting pot of nationalities due to the country's history of colonization: Spanish, Chinese, Malaysian. Approximately 300 years after Magellan's discovery of the Philippines, Spanish friars had Christianized most of the native people and decreed that they be given Spanish surnames. Thus many of my Filipino friends were named Gonzalez, Gomez, or Velazquez. Their first names were Pablo instead of Paul, José instead of Joseph. However, the friars were not successful in converting the Muslims in Mindanao, the large southernmost island.

I had two best friends at the time. One was a Spanish Jew from Syria named Eli Halila, his ancestors most probably driven out of Spain during the Spanish Inquisition. My other best friend, Gilbert Dee, was of Chinese ancestry. His father was president of the Bank of China. When I last saw him, Gilbert himself had an executive position at the Bank of China. I also had a Spanish friend named Alejandro Aboitiz, who later immigrated to Australia. Other Filipino friends included Oscar Barrera, Joaquin Quintos III, and Juanito Pagkaliwagan.

On weekends most people were family-oriented, but my friends and I would sometimes go bowling or to the movies. When we started noticing girls, we would have parties in each other's homes. We'd turn on the record player and dance. It wasn't easy to meet girls, since we went to all-boys schools. We mainly had to rely on the sisters of classmates, who would invite their own friends to parties. Still, I think going to a single-sex school is good for most children and allows them more freedom intellectually and athletically—and it kept our minds on our studies most of the time!

> *I think going to a single-sex school is good
> for most children and allows them more freedom
> intellectually and athletically—and it kept our minds
> on our studies most of the time!*

I learned to drive in my dad's Ford convertible and got my license at the age of sixteen. The system was corrupt; you would get a license by paying someone a fee, without even taking a driver's test. One of my father's friends said, "I'll get your son a license." He taught me to drive, and he was a good teacher. In the Philippines, few cars stop for stop signs. One day I got caught going through one and got a ticket. The traffic ticket system was a racket, too. If you gave the policeman five pesos, he might just tear up the ticket.

Once I got my license I would drop my father off at work, then use the car to drive my mother around for groceries and errands. On weekends I got permission to use the car. If you could drive your girlfriend around in a car, that was a big thing. It was difficult to find a part-time job to earn gas or pocket money, though. Filipinos did most of the menial jobs, which paid little. My parents would give me money for meals, movies, or clothing if I needed it. They didn't have a lot to give, but we rarely felt deprived.

Unlike today, there was hardly any alcohol at parties. The adults might have wine, liquor, or beer, but the only drinks the kids had were Coke or Pepsi. Our parents would stay around to keep an eye on us. They would always serve home-cooked food—there was no pizza in those days—and would enjoy watching us dance, usually sitting in an adjoining room where it wasn't as noisy. We loved American music, mostly country and western. We'd listen to records, and people would bring their own to parties. Elvis Presley didn't come on the scene until after I was in college, the Beatles even later. Xavier Cugat was popular. My parents were kind of reserved, so we didn't have as many parties as some families, but we did have them occasionally.

From visiting classmates' homes, I learned that there was quite a disparity in wealth among us. The rich families usually had fancier parties, and maybe better food. But as we approached our senior year of high school, it also became clear that some of my rich classmates wouldn't have to worry about college or job prospects; places were being held for them at their family businesses.

It became clear that some of my rich classmates wouldn't have to worry about college or job prospects; places were being held for them at their family businesses.

I, on the other hand, had to give it some thought. Sometimes I'd remember the Japanese propaganda newsreels I'd seen in China—the armaments and war planes, and the factories where they were built. I had an inkling that I would go into engineering. For example, I liked to work on my dad's car. Sometimes he'd come home from work and say, "There's a knocking sound somewhere." So I would go under the hood of the car and try to find out what was loose. In those days, a car was so simple. You could almost repair it yourself if you had the right tools.

I was interested in going to the University of the Philippines, which was larger and co-ed and had an engineering department, but I ended up going to college at De La Salle. As I wasn't

48

Filipino I wasn't entitled to discounted tuition at the University of the Philippines, so it would have been too expensive. I entered the mechanical engineering program at De La Salle.

My high school graduation photo from De La Salle High School, 1954.
I am in my Philippine Military Training uniform;
I was the first sergeant for my platoon.

De La Salle had an American-style high school graduation ceremony, and even a junior and senior prom. We all got dressed up and went to the dance at the Army-Navy Club. I took the sister of one of my friends, a nice girl named Betty Young. I had few girlfriends—a couple of girls who were crushes, you might say. But I was on the quiet side. I asked myself, "Why am I so shy?" I wished I were more outgoing, able to go up and introduce myself to girls. But then I met Conchita.

Conchita and I met at a neighborhood birthday party. I was nineteen years old and a first-year college student. I was attracted to her at first sight: she was beautiful and petite. I knew she was a friend of my classmates and lived close by, but I didn't know her name. (I've always been terrible with names.) All I remembered was that my friends had told me that she was nineteen years old and a first-year college student, just like me. I said to a friend, "I like that girl over there, the nineteen-year-old." That is what I called her, Number Nineteen.

Her name was Concepción Yupangco, but everyone called her Conchita. She was the youngest of six children, with a noticeably light complexion because she had more Chinese blood, maybe, than Filipino blood. (Yupangco is a Chinese name.) In later years, we would kid her father that he must have been a pirate. When the Spanish ruled the Philippines for 300 years, their biggest enemies were Chinese pirates who raided the coastal towns and cities.

Conchita was a quiet girl and I was on the shy side, but she was so attractive that I forced myself to introduce myself that night. I approached and asked her to dance. I thought she might not respond, but surprisingly she stood up and we danced. Now, dancing in those days wasn't like dancing today, where there's a lot of action. It was more of a moving embrace; we called it slow drag. So we were remarkably close, face to face, and we got to talk quietly.

*Conchita and me dancing at a house party in the Philippines.
Everyone had parties in their homes, and danced to music on
a record player. We were dating at this time.*

She was studying business administration at the University of the Philippines. I worked up the courage to ask where she lived, and she gave me the address of her dorm. Basically, I fell in love with Conchita right away. She was extremely sweet, and she wanted a boyfriend who would protect her, whom she could trust but could also have fun with.

Basically, I fell in love with Conchita right away.

Once I got to know Conchita, any other girlfriends meant nothing to me. At first she had lots of boys interested in her, so there was some competition. Of course, she enjoyed the chase, and having the attention of many boys. I knew that other guys were interested in her, but I didn't get into arguments over it. We just kind of let things fall as they did, and eventually she gave them the signal that she preferred me. I was happy that I ended up being her top choice.

I started visiting Conchita at the University of the Philippines, about a half-hour away by bus. It was a nonsectarian school, with single-sex dorms. I was only allowed in the lobby of her YWCA dorm, so usually we would walk around the campus. It was becoming more common for women at that time to go to college, though most were still taking courses such as home economics or liberal arts. One of Conchita's sisters had gone to secretarial school, but all she had learned was how to type and take shorthand. So Conchita's mother told her she had to go to university. The tuition wasn't expensive for Filipino citizens.

I learned that during the war Conchita's family had to evacuate from Manila and escape into the provinces. To afford whatever lay ahead, her mother sold some of their prized possessions: jewelry, furniture, clothing. Evacuees often were robbed by the Japanese or by locals, who assumed (rightly) that these families were carrying all their money and valuables on their backs. To avoid being robbed, Conchita's parents hid their stash not on themselves but on Conchita, their tiny youngest daughter. They took a train to the home of a kindly relative who was manager of a cement factory, and he gave them shelter. In those war years they endured food shortages and other privations, but they were generally safe. Afterward they moved back to Manila, where their home was empty but intact.

Conchita and I were interested in each other, but we weren't allowed to go on a date by ourselves. Her parents said we had to have a chaperone. They would make a cousin or a niece or someone else accompany us. When we were with our families, we could never put our arms around each other. We would sit apart, talking but not close.

Usually Conchita would invite her nephew as a chaperone. He was just eight or nine years old. He'd sit in the back seat of my dad's car, and we'd bribe him with popcorn or candy. While he was chewing away, we'd get nice and cozy in the front seat. In those days cars had bench seats, so I would drive and Conchita would sit right next to me, shoulder-to-shoulder, holding my hand. No seatbelts in those days. And our "chaperone" would be reading a comic book, keeping himself entertained.

It was kind of an interesting game. One time Conchita and I were walking down a busy downtown street to go to a movie. And lo and behold, her father came walking down the other way. He was a retired Navy engineer, older than my parents, and liked to take long walks. I said, "Uh oh." But he greeted me and was genuinely nice. We were worried he would talk to Conchita's mother, but he didn't say anything. And we didn't tell him that we were going to a movie. If he had found out we would have gotten in trouble, because everyone knew that going to the movies was just an excuse to make out! Going out with your girlfriend or boyfriend without a chaperone was like eating the forbidden fruit.

Conchita would take the bus home from college on weekends so she could do her laundry and we could see each other, as her family lived close to mine. My brother dated a friend of hers, and we spent as much time together as we could. I had a home phone but she didn't, so she had to go to a neighbor's house or to a public phone to call me so we could make plans.

When Conchita and I got more serious about one another, my grades improved. Funnily enough, her grades did just the opposite. I'd help her with her accounting homework, and she passed the course. She was intelligent—that I knew—but our relationship was a distraction for her. On the other hand, I was able to graduate with honors.

Conchita's father had been in the Philippine Navy, which fought with the US Navy in World War II and been decimated by the Japanese. During the war he'd worked as an engineer in the boiler room of a cargo ship. He retired a few years after the war. Her mother was a homemaker. I would consider them middle class. I got to know them through visits to their home and meals together. Conchita's mother insisted on speaking Spanish as a point of cultural pride. Spanish was the language spoken by rich Spanish-Filipinos from the Spanish colonial days.

De La Salle College didn't have aeronautical engineering, but I wanted to pursue mechanical engineering to begin anyway. As my studies progressed, I was still interested in aeronautics, so I enrolled at the Far Eastern Aeronautics School (FEATI), founded in 1946 in Manila, to take a few aeronautical courses as electives—like Theory of Flight and Aircraft Propeller Design.

Meanwhile, I continued with track and running. The first Asian Games, held every four years for athletes from all over Asia, had been hosted in New Delhi in 1950. The second Games were going to take place in Manila in 1954, and I badly wanted to qualify. I was a sophomore by that time, and I embarked on a rigid training regime. My races were the 400, 800, and 1,500 meters. I was selected to represent De La Salle College in the trials to make the national team and competed against hundreds of runners from other colleges, but I wasn't selected. That was the end of my racing career, you might say, or my dreams of one.

However, I had spent so much time training that my studies were falling behind. I had to make a choice between books or track. I figured that books are for life, while track was only for three years. I considered myself an average IQ student; I wasn't a genius. So I had to spend more time studying than most students. I didn't give sports up completely; I still ran and played soccer. But in retrospect it was good that I didn't make it to the Asian Games, as I began to do quite well academically.

I had to make a choice between books or track. I figured that books are for life, while track was only for three years.

I developed a method of study that worked for me—and it didn't involve taking notes. I noticed that the minute teachers would start writing on the chalkboard, students would put their heads down and take notes. But I would listen. My handwriting is bad, and I hated taking notes. But soon I noticed that I got more out of the lectures than they did. A friend would later say, "I wrote this note down. I don't understand what happened." And I would explain, "This is what the teacher was trying to say." I concentrated in class, and then if I didn't understand I'd put my hand up and ask questions. The other students didn't ask any questions—they were just taking notes. I learned more because I asked a lot of dumb questions. I wasn't afraid to ask.

When I got home from class, I would open my textbook and review what the teacher had just taught. It was all in the textbook, anyway. So why should you even write it down? Between what I heard and what I read, it all came together. As opposed to high school, I began to do well academically in college. I enjoyed most of the courses and spent many hours each day studying. As a result of my method—listening to the lectures, no notetaking but studying the textbook—I advanced more quickly than other students.

I remember March 17, 1957, very well. I had just recently graduated from college. That day I was at a formal luncheon at the invitation of the Philippine Society of Mechanical Engineers (PSME). It was an awards ceremony, and I was one of the awardees. For my advanced studies in mechanical engineering at De La Salle, I received a special citation and a medal, which I still have.

The luncheon was interrupted by a bulletin over the public address system announcing that Ramon Magsaysay, the president of the Philippines, had just been killed in an airplane crash. He was something of a national hero, best known for successfully defeating the communist-led Hukbalahap movement or suppressing them to the point of insignificance. He had been elected president in 1953.

I admired Magsaysay very much, because you might say he was one of the few honest figures around. As a student of world history, it seemed to me that most politicians had blemishes on their records—as many of our past US presidents have. But Ramon Magsaysay was especially good. He was a popular president and seemed forthright and dedicated.

The audience was distraught, as was the country. The reaction at the time was like that of the American public when President John F. Kennedy was assassinated—the sense that Magsaysay had died too young, and with so much good left to do. What had been a wonderful day for me was now a sad day for the Philippines. It was a very strange feeling.

Magsaysay's funeral procession wound through the main streets of Manila. We gathered to watch from the apartment of Conchita's sister. Sadly, his promise was not carried by subsequent presidents, the most famous (or infamous) of whom was Ferdinand Marcos, who came to power in 1965. Marcos's wife, Imelda, became an international celebrity, most notably for her 3,000 pairs of shoes. The Filipinos were great lovers of luxury, and people went crazy for Imelda, even donating shoes to her so they could brag to their friends about it.

There was a great discrepancy of wealth in the Philippines. Most of the wealth was handed down from generation to generation. The rich kids had jobs waiting for them at their family businesses, even homes provided for them, while the rest of us had little opportunity to advance ourselves. Many of my classmates from well-established families had connections; it seems the rich and powerful somehow take care of one another. It was not a place where middle-class kids like me were able to work their way up and found their own companies—the "American dream."

I began to consider moving abroad to pursue engineering. It became clear that the Philippines would not be a land of opportunity for me. About a half-dozen of my classmates would move abroad for this same reason. I believed that in America it would be just the opposite: whether you are rich or poor, if you can do the job you will be hired. I have found that there is relatively little nepotism here in the US.

Unlike in the Philippines, where there was much nepotism, I believed that in America, whether you are rich or poor, if you can do the job you will be hired.

Over the years I'd hear about classmates or friends in the Philippines who eventually left their family businesses because they couldn't handle working there. Either they were just too spoiled or they didn't care for the business; they would rather do something else. But most wealthy families were able to keep their offspring in the country to find success in the family businesses.

I didn't talk much with my parents about my career plans. They were busy trying to earn a living themselves. My father was a particularly good accountant, but I think because of office politics and maybe his personality, he had problems keeping a job. When he was out of work, obviously it was difficult for the family. It seemed we were always in a tight financial situation.

We had come to Manila with my dad's job at Everett Shipping. But then he got a job as an accountant with the US Air Force at Clark Air Force Base. I assume it was better paid. But the Air Force was in the process of moving out of the Philippines and returning its bases to the Philippine government. When the base closed, my father had to look for another job. He ended up working for a bus company. Three jobs in ten years—not a good sign. But it was just one of those things—jobs weren't plentiful and were difficult to get, especially for a non-Filipino.

My mother handled money better than my father, who tended to be an impulse buyer. She would say, "We're having some issues, so we must watch it. Do not spend too much on clothing," or on this or that. We weren't the only family to experience financial instability, but my mother was capable—especially after her experiences during World War II—and we rarely went without the necessities.

There was one time, however, when our financial situation affected me greatly. My father was unemployed, and it became clear that he couldn't pay the college tuition for my brother John and me. He sent me to speak to the dean of De La Salle College and explain our situation—that he was looking for a job and couldn't cover our tuition, and that we might have to drop out for a while. I was nervous and even ashamed, but I went to talk to the dean, a Christian brother. He listened to my plight and said, "Go back to school, and we'll worry about the money later." He allowed me to continue my classes without any disruption. It was genuinely nice of him.

The question of the unpaid tuition bothered me for years. Did my father ever pay back the money? I was too embarrassed to ask. But later in life I would find my own method of settling my debts at De La Salle.

The shame of that moment wasn't something I ever wanted to relive. It made me even more certain that the "New World," as I called it—America, Canada, South America—held greater opportunity for me. Most middle-class families, if they had a chance, would try to go abroad. I felt we had more of a future in the New World. My parents were supportive of the move. They knew that the future lay in going abroad. We didn't have the connections to make a good living in the Philippines, which might have contributed to my father's career difficulties. It was understood that if I could make a life in the New World, my family would follow.

> *It was understood that if I could make a life in the New World, my family would follow.*

I didn't know many people who had moved overseas. In fact, I felt like a pioneer in my family. But I would have a fellow explorer—my brother John. Even though we were fourteen months apart, for some reason, my father and mother decided to start us in kindergarten at the same time. We went all through school together, though in college he went into chemical engineering and I went into mechanical engineering.

John and I had many of the same friends and got along well. He was also studious, though not as much as I was. And he was a bit more open, with maybe more friends than I had. We were both on the shy side, academic, and interested in sports. He was a swimmer.

My graduation photo, 1956. I graduated cum laude
from De La Salle University in Manila.

Our graduation from De La Salle College was a cap-and-gown occasion. I graduated cum laude. It was a big thing for me. My father and mother gave us a party; we invited friends (mainly neighbors) and classmates. Conchita was invited, but we didn't invite her parents, since our families weren't intertwined at that time. I only saw them if I visited her at home.

While John and I made plans to move abroad, I worked for one of my professors at a sugar mill as an unpaid intern to gain some work experience. I also took additional aeronautical courses at FEATI. I was awarded a scholarship for one semester because of my good grades.

Me with my family at home in Manila. Probably just before leaving for Canada, 1957.

*Me in the backyard of our family home
in Manila, c. 1956.*

The question now was where John and I would move—the USA, Canada, England, or Australia?

First I approached the US Embassy to apply for a visa, and they turned me down. Well, they didn't turn me down; they said, "Yes, you can apply. But the wait is quite long." So I asked, "How long will it be: a year, two years?"

The agent said, "I hate to tell you this, but it's going to be ninety years."

"Why?" I asked.

He told me, "There's a long list of Chinese citizens who want to come to the United States." Shanghai had fallen under communist rule, and I was now considered a Chinese citizen. I was disappointed but thought, "All right, I'll try to go to Australia." However, I learned that Australia had a whites-only policy; they were only open to immigrants from Europe and the US.

England was my third choice. But the country was still the postwar era and hadn't recovered fully. The aircraft industry was prominent in the UK because they were a leading builder of the first jet airliner, the Comet, and were far advanced in the aeronautical field. But the available jobs were for British citizens. I couldn't get a visa. So: Canada!

When I went to the Canadian embassy, they asked about my educational background. I said, "I just graduated from college, with a degree in mechanical engineering and some aeronautical courses." So they said, "Send us that information and fill out this application form." I filled it out, and within two or three weeks I received a letter that said I had been approved for immigration to Canada once I tested negative for TB. The embassy gave me the paperwork to be a landed immigrant, which meant that I was legally allowed to enter Canada and live and work there with no time limit.

I knew little about Canada. The Canadian Embassy counselor gave me all kinds of literature about the country. The aircraft industry at that time was concentrated in Toronto and Montreal, so I picked Toronto, basically because it was English-speaking. I typed up two letters on my typewriter, as businesslike as possible, and sent them to two Toronto companies: Orenda Engines and Avro Aircraft Ltd, makers of jet engines and airframes, respectively. A few weeks later I received letters from both saying that they could not offer me a job until I arrived in Canada.

The freighter tickets to the US were about $200 each, the equivalent of about $2,000 today. That was a lot of money. My parents had to borrow the funds to pay for them.

The freighter route depended on its cargo. Our freighter, the *Hoegh Silverspray*, was delivering Philippine lumber to San Francisco. It was a nonstop, 21-day trip. That was quick, but I missed out seeing some of the places I would like to have seen. Yet if I'd taken a passenger liner, the ticket would have cost thousands of dollars—and that was out of the question. There were flights from the Philippines to the United States on Pan Am,

Northwest, and Philippine Airlines, but in those days one had to fly from island to island. Planes would fly from the Philippines to Guam, then Guam to Honolulu, and finally Honolulu to the United States, for example. And these were piston engine planes, not jet engines, so they were noisier and more turbulent and had to fly lower. They were also prohibitively expensive.

A 1960 photo of the steamship on which my brother and I traveled from Manila to the port in San Francisco.

Manila had changed during the ten years I'd lived there. It was a brand-new city. The scars of war were beginning to vanish. The rubble and devastation had been cleared, and streets and infrastructure had been rebuilt. I didn't have a television, but people were starting to get them. There was a US Army television station in the Philippines for their service people, but the only program I remember was the Arthur Godfrey talk show, sponsored by Chesterfield cigarettes. Godfrey would talk up Chesterfields—how good the taste was! Soon after I left for Canada, my mother and father won an Admiral black-and-white television set in a bingo game. They sent a photo of it to me.

I took two suitcases to the New World. One was filled with summer clothing—which is all that I had, coming from a tropical place. Once it was autumn in Canada, I had to buy heavier clothing. The other suitcase was filled with my textbooks, which I have to this day. I also brought my diploma, my thesis on gas turbine engines, and my trusty engineering slide rule. As there were no calculators at the time, that was an important instrument.

I took two suitcases to Canada. One was filled with summer clothing—which is all that I had—and the other was filled with my textbooks.

We had a small going-away party. Conchita wasn't happy that I was moving to Canada, and I was sad that we would be separated. It was a teary parting. But we didn't discuss marriage then. Conchita and I promised that we would write letters and stay in touch. Maybe, as a twenty-two-year-old, I thought that I would meet a prettier, smarter, kinder girl in the New World. But that would not be the case—no one compared to Conchita. Over the next two years, the distance between us only made our hearts grow fonder.

John and me at Manila Bay, just before leaving the Philippines, 1957.

Once John and I boarded the boat, the passage was strangely uneventful. It was smooth sailing all the way to San Francisco. In fact, we said to each other, "Gosh, wish it would roughen up a little bit!" But in those days, ships were very conscious about storms, which could be extremely dangerous. We mostly just sat around. There was no television, no radio. We made no stops. All we saw was water. We passed by Iwo Jima and Midway islands, historic battle sites during World War II. I plotted the trip on the globe as we went along.

My brother John and me on the Hoegh Silverspray,
traveling to San Francisco from the Philippines.

The other passengers weren't interesting to two young single men. Mostly Protestant clergy taking a leave from their missionary work in India, they would return to home and families for a few months and then resume their overseas posts. They were mostly in their thirties and unmarried; we had good conversations, but that was about it. However, I will never forget a nice elderly couple returning to Canada from Asia. After hearing that we were on our way to Canada for the first time, not knowing anyone there and not having jobs, they knew it was going to be a struggle for us to get established. They gave us some money for our journey, about $100 as I recall. It could have been $20 or $30, but whatever it was seemed like a lot to us in those days.

We ate our meals at the captain's table. The food was quite simple. Toward the end of the trip, as we were approaching San Francisco, the captain asked, "Do you want me to wake you up at 4 am?" "Why?" I asked. He said, "Well, we'll be entering the harbor at 4 in the morning, and you'll want to see Alcatraz." I didn't even know what Alcatraz was, but I said, "Sure." When we got up, it was cold and damp even though it was June! We weren't used to the chilly weather. We sailed by Alcatraz; I might have understood that it was a prison. But when Conchita and I went to San Francisco on vacation decades later, we made it a point to visit Alcatraz, which was no longer a prison but now a tourist attraction.

A few years before I left Manila I had constructed the crystal radio set illustrated in the Cub Scout guide, on the page I'd ripped out and brought with me from Shanghai. Often I had put on my earphones and gone to bed listening to music or the news from the Clark Air Force Base station before falling off to sleep. Crystal radios didn't require electricity or a charger; they were self-powered, which made them convenient and inexpensive. The sound was only loud enough to hear with earphones. People would string up antennas in trees to try for a better signal; you'd use the tuner to adjust the current and frequency to get a radio station. My set was built on a wooden base. I was able to get a solid-state diode, and I wound the magnet wire around a cardboard tube. I didn't really understand how a crystal radio set worked when I made it, but after my college engineering courses I did. The elements were rudimentary, but the conversion from radio frequency to audio waves was quite sophisticated. It seemed almost magical that you could make a working radio from such simple elements.

As we sat on the deck of the freighter crossing the Pacific, I told my brother about my idea to make and market crystal radio sets in Canada. We didn't have jobs and had only a few hundred dollars between us, and I liked the idea of starting my own business. In those days, crystal radios were popular in the Philippines, and I thought there would be a similar demand in a big country like Canada.

*I would have to think of another way to make a name
for myself in the New World.*

But I would learn that Canada had plentiful electricity. Every house had light, and heat, and a phone. Nearly everyone had a television set and a radio, even a car. My crystal radio business idea had been naïve. I would have to think of another way to make a name for myself in the New World.

TORONTO

While the boat passage had been uneventful, I was excited that my overland journey to Toronto held the promise of adventure. I arrived in San Francisco at about 4 am on a pass-through visa, allowing me to travel through the US to enter Canada. After John and I went through immigration we visited with my cousin Francisco, whose family I'd lost track of after leaving Shanghai. His father—my father's brother—had applied for Portuguese citizenship during the war, so he and his family hadn't been interned. After the communists took over, the family had left Shanghai and emigrated to Macau, at that time a Portuguese colony. A few years later they were somehow granted visas to the United States. In a way they were still just settling in, struggling to earn a living, but they were safe and well situated.

Francisco met us at the docks, and we walked around the city—and of course through Chinatown. We may have eaten there—I don't recall it well. What I do remember is walking on San Francisco's Skid Row. There were drunks staggering around on the sidewalks or sleeping on the pavement, people begging for money and lining up at a soup kitchen. I was used to the homeless and beggars on the streets of Shanghai, but I was shocked to see them in the United States—white people especially, as most of the destitute in Shanghai were Chinese. We had never heard about *this* America. We thought the streets of America would be paved in gold!

I was used to the homeless and beggars on the streets of Shanghai, but I was shocked to see them in the United States. We thought the streets of America would be paved in gold!

69

I visited a travel agent, who gave me options for getting to Toronto. A one-way airplane flight was $120 (the equivalent of about $1,200 today). The train was $99 (about $1,000). We chose the train, which would give us a chance to see some of the United States. But our main concern was saving money! Between my brother and me, we'd left the Philippines with $1,000 at the most. We were conscious of repaying the debt my parents had incurred with a loan shark in Manila to help fund our move.

We traveled on the California Zephyr railway line, billed as "the most talked about train in America" at its launch in 1949. The route from Oakland to Chicago was designed to pass through the most spectacular scenery during daylight hours. We traveled in one of the "Vista Dome" trains, which consisted of three coaches, a lounge, and a sleeper-observation car in addition to the normal baggage, dining, and sleeping cars. The train hostesses were known as Zephyrettes. During the day we enjoyed views of mountains, rivers, valleys, and snow: landscapes we had only seen in books. At night the train traveled through the flatlands. During stopovers we'd hop off and buy sandwiches, or we'd eat in the dining car. We slept in our seats.

We met a nice American couple from San Francisco. I asked, "Why are you traveling to Chicago?" The man told us, "I came to pick up a car." From Chicago they would head to Detroit to pick up their new car from the factory, then drive home to avoid paying the costly car freight.

When we got to Chicago I called the sister of one of the Christian brothers from De La Salle, who lived there. We figured out how to get to her home on the city's famous "L" elevated railway trains, and she and her husband served us dinner. She told us, "You've got to have American steaks"—which we very much enjoyed.

We were having a wonderful time. My only disappointment was that I had lost my treasured Sheaffer fountain pen somewhere along the journey. It was an American-made pen that I'd bought from the PX at Clark Air Force Base in Manila when my father worked there. I'd gone through four years of college with that pen and somehow had misplaced it, maybe when writing an aerogram to Conchita or my parents. A pen was the engineer's main means of communication at the time, used constantly in writing and design. Yes, there were typewriters. But we would scribble notes on pieces of paper, then give them to secretaries to type so that we wouldn't have any grammatical or spelling errors—because most engineers are good at calculations but poor writers of anything!

Later, when I worked in the United States, every engineering department had at least one or two secretaries to type out reports, letters, etc. In fact, a decade or more later I mentioned to my secretary in Clifton Springs, New York, that I had lost my favorite Shaeffer pen. She was able to find that same type of pen and surprised me with it as a present. Such a thoughtful gift! I still have it.

The next day we returned to the Chicago train station to board the Canadian National Railway's "Maple Leaf." Our first stop in Canada was in Sarnia, Ontario, where we went through immigration. About three hours from Toronto, Sarnia is the chemical capital of Canada, so John—a chemical engineer—might have recognized the name. From there the train continued to Toronto.

I was elated by my first impressions of Toronto. It was so clean, and such a rich cultural city. The people were mostly of British heritage at that time, but there were many diverse neighborhoods: a Chinatown, a Greektown, a Little Italy. It was the middle of summer, and the city's many public parks were full of greenery, trees, flowers, and people.

I was elated by my first impressions of Toronto.
It was so clean, and such a rich cultural city.

Finding a place to live was tricky. We went to the immigrant assistance office and obtained a list of places for rent. We just went through the list, taking streetcars or trains around the city. The first place we visited was horrible. It was a boarding house, a popular accommodation at the time. Some boarding houses might have as many as six people boarding in private rooms, with everyone sharing a common kitchen and one or two bathrooms. I distinctly remember that in the first one we visited, the bedsheets weren't very clean. So we looked up another place, a row house in an Italian neighborhood downtown. The couple who owned the place could hardly speak English, but their grown son, a schoolteacher, lived with them and spoke English very well. The husband was a janitor for a factory, and his wife took care of the boarders. The house was spotless, and the rent was ridiculously low—$15 a week. That included two meals a day, breakfast and supper, even on the weekends—and the owner would sometimes even wash my laundry! It was amazing how cheap it was, but it still seemed like a lot because I wasn't working. My limited amount of money was beginning to dwindle.

We started applying for jobs. Within two or three weeks my brother was on his way back to Sarnia, having secured a job there. I was still looking, directing my focus toward aircraft engine or aircraft manufacturing companies only. I interviewed at a company called Lucas Rotax Ltd., which manufactured jet engine fuel control systems for the Iroquois Jet Engine, manufactured by Orenda Engines for the CF-105 Arrow Interceptor. It was located in the Toronto suburb of Scarborough. They asked simple questions and reviewed my college transcript and the thesis on gas turbine engines that I had brought from the Philippines. I was thrilled when they offered me a job as a development engineer at $4,999 Canadian dollars per year.

The CF-105 was designed to fly at Mach 2 speed at an altitude of 50,000 feet. Its mission was to intercept Soviet bombers flying across the North Pole to attack Canadian and US targets. The first Arrow was rolled out to the public on October 4, 1957. Unfortunately, this debut was all but ignored in the international press, as it happened on the same day as the launch of Sputnik 1, the first Earth satellite, by the Soviet Union. Nonetheless, it was an exciting project and an exciting time in aviation.

I was assigned to work with other engineers on the CF-105's main engine control and the afterburner controls. My job was to redesign certain control valve features to match changes in the engine fuel control schedules, as the engine performance was being upgraded. Since I began during the summer months when many employees were on vacation, Lucas Rotax didn't know quite where to put me, so they had me do some production work, testing hydraulic filters to make sure they met certain quality requirements. After a few weeks I was put into an engineering department where we performed testing on prototype control valves. All engineering products start in design and drafting; once the parts are made by the manufacturing department, they're vetted by test engineers, who simulate the specific conditions that will be seen on the airplane.

I worked under an engineer who instructed me in how the various controls worked. But the airplane engine has many different controls: the turbines, the afterburners. And each control has different engineers, so I often had to go to several engineers to understand how to test a single control. I was surprised that the company even had German engineers, as Germans were still unpopular a decade after the war. There were also English and Polish employees. The European employees had emigrated to Canada shortly after the war because there were no jobs in their home countries; they were displaced people, like me. Thus we had a lot of common interests and discussed our wartime experiences. I was the only employee from Asia. The chief engineer for whom I worked was from Poland, an EX-RAF pilot who had flown Spitfires against German aircraft during WWII, notably during the Battle of Britain.

The airplane engine has many different controls, and each control has different engineers. So I often had to go to several engineers to understand how to test a control.

The moment I got a job, I started sending money to the Philippines—as did my brother. My parents were able to pay off the loan shark within a few months. I was really pleased. After that I began to save up for a car. I only needed to put down ten percent to have it financed. I'd been using the subways and streetcars and had to make several transfers to get to Lucas Rotax in Scarborough. I remember waiting for streetcars in the snow. But before the long Toronto winter really set in, I had my own brand-new car, a 1958 four-door English Ford Zephyr in Kenilworth Blue!

I had expected freezing weather in Toronto, but the subzero temperatures and deep snow were something I could never have imagined. I installed a block heater in my car engine to keep the oil temperature from going below 40 degrees Fahrenheit so that early in the morning the engine would start instantly. The heater was installed into one of the frost plugs of the engine block. You'd plug the electric cord from the block heater into an electric outlet and leave it on all night. In the morning—unplug, and the engine started effortlessly.

I would say that I didn't have the typical immigrant experience for that time. In those days, immigrants anywhere in the world were treated as second-class citizens. There was always a certain amount of distance between Canadian nationals and immigrants—like my Italian landlords—who were mostly in the trades and often didn't even learn the language. I was lucky, because I had an education and a job. I spoke English, was familiar with British culture and foods, and was a Christian. All these factors allowed me to integrate into Canadian society without any difficulty.

> *I spoke English, was familiar with British culture and foods, and was a Christian. All these factors allowed me to integrate into Canadian society without any difficulty.*

I'd never had any insecurities or worries about moving to Canada, and before long I was working. I was not financially distressed. I didn't spend too much money on frivolous things in those days. I would deposit my paycheck in my account at the Royal Band of Canada across the street. My first credit cards were from Diners Club, mainly for restaurants, and Shell Oil, for gas.

I lived at the Italian boarding house for just three or four months, until I got my car. The house was simply too far from work. I moved to another boarding house in Scarborough, close to where I worked. It was owned by an older British couple. I was in an upstairs bedroom, and the other two bedrooms were occupied by the wife's mother and brother. There was a basement rented out to a fellow Lucas Rotax employee and his wife and child. I paid $18 a week for food and lodging, and the landlady would even do my laundry every once in a while if she saw it piling up!

The landlady's brother was an interesting person—a nice guy, but he had a drinking problem. Their mother was sickly. When the owners took a trip to Florida for two weeks, I offered to help the brother take care of his mother. But one night he drank so much that I took the wine bottle and poured the contents down the drain so he would think he'd finished it. When the landlady got back, she asked, "How did John behave?" "Not very well," I said, and told her what I'd done. She thanked me for taking care of him.

I wasn't a drinker, but at Lucas Rotax I joined the bowling team, and during matches we'd drink wine or beer. I found it amusing that if we drank hard liquor we'd have Canadian Club whiskey. I thought it tasted terrible, but with Canada Dry ginger ale it was great.

When working at Lucas Rotax, I spent late nights either at the company site or at home educating myself on the diverse types of controls. There was a night shift, so the building was open and I could use the equipment at any hour. I was so interested in the product that I learned quite quickly. A lot of the engineers were single, like me, in their mid-twenties or early thirties, so we had a lot in common and would go out together occasionally. When I could find the time, I'd write to Conchita and my family.

My brother John worked for a company in Sarnia called Polysar, which made synthetic rubber for automotive tires. We'd get together every other month or so, in either city. But during the long winters, on the weekends, I didn't do much. I might listen to the radio or read a book.

I loved my car. At the time, people asked, "Why'd you buy a four-door instead of a two-door?" I said, "Well, I'm preparing for a family." I was thinking ahead. And in fact, during my first few months in Canada, I decided that Conchita was the girl for me. From the very beginning, she came on strong in her letters. She believed that we would be together forever and wanted assurances from me. Though I continued to write, I did not yet make a firm commitment on my end.

During my first few months in Canada, I decided
that Conchita was the girl for me.

I did pick up a new sport in Canada: skiing. There were some small ski slopes in Toronto. I didn't take lessons, just purchased some ski boots and skis and learned by trial and error. The boots were made in Austria and required quite a bit of effort to lace up. In those days, you pulled yourself up the mountain with a tow bar. Once you got up to the peak, you'd release it and head down the slopes. Skiing down the hill, I felt I had come a very long way from my life in the Philippines!

As the months went by, I became sure that Conchita was my one and only. Our bond had continued to grow through our letters, and I wanted to marry her. As I was thousands of miles away, I proposed to her by Canadian Aerogram, and I wrote in my proposal that I would also be writing to her parents and mine, letting them know of my intentions. Once I got her acceptance by mail, it was only a question of how and when.

*Conchita's graduation photo from
University of the Philippines, 1957.*

My parents and my sister, now in high school, were also planning to move to Canada. So I suggested that they meet and talk
with Conchita's parents in Manila and propose that she travel
with them. It was the first time they had met, and fortunately her
parents were receptive to the idea. I told my brother of my plans.
"I figured you were going to marry her," he said. He had also had
a girlfriend back home, but he married a Canadian a year or two
later, a high school student.

There were some complications with my plan. First and most
importantly, I was now out of work. Due to mounting costs,
technical delays, and Canadian government deficits, the prime
minister of Canada cancelled CF-105 production on February
20, 1959, a day that became known in the Canadian aviation
industry as "Black Friday." On that day Avro Aircraft, Orenda
Engines, and Lucas Rotax, along with many other companies
associated with design and manufacture of the CF-105, laid off
thousands of employees. We heard over the company public
address system that the company would be shuttering—and just

like that, everyone who worked there, both management and staff, was out of a job. I wanted to stay in Canada but had trouble finding another job. As I was about to get married, I thought I had better expand my search to the United States as well.

Just like that, everyone who worked
at Lucas Rotax was out of a job.

At the time there was a great need for engineers in the United States, and several US companies had advertised jobs in Canadian newspapers. I was able to set up a few interviews. One was with Pitney Bowes, the metered mail company, for a job based in New York. I wasn't that interested, as it wasn't an aircraft company, but I went for the experience and the free trip to New York City—my first airplane flight. It was memorable because I flew on the famous British Vickers Viscount, the first turbo prop. Prior to that, airplanes had internal combustion engines, but the Air Force developed what is known as a jet engine–driven, or turbine, propeller plane. An innovative airplane, it was much quieter, with less vibration, and at the time America didn't have anything similar. The Vickers Viscount seated no more than 100 people, and its range was somewhat limited, so it was for regional travel only.

I declined the Pitney Bowes job and instead accepted a position at Ronson Hydraulics, based in Charlotte, North Carolina. The company made hydraulic controls including valves for a variety of military and commercial aircraft, and Ajax and Hercules guided missiles, and had come to Toronto for interviews. Ronson would take care of the US visa. But by the time of our wedding, the paperwork and immigration forms hadn't yet been finalized—and until it was, I had no income.

The second complication was that when Conchita first applied for a visa, the Canadian consulate declined her application because we were not yet married. So I contacted the member of parliament who represented my district. "I'll take care of it," he said. He gave me the necessary paperwork and his letter of recommendation. Based on those, Conchita's visa was granted. However, I had to post a $1,000 bond in case she came and we didn't get married, and she had to be deported. I didn't know that I could go to a bail bond agent to borrow the money, so I withdrew $1,000 from my savings. Of course, once I presented the marriage certificate, the Canadian government would send me a refund. But at the time I was between jobs, and my savings were diminishing. The bond was a fortune to me!

A third complication was that Conchita's "fiancée visa" required that our marriage take place within a month of her arrival. I called a local Catholic church and told them our circumstances. They said they could accommodate our wedding, as we would be such a small party. A week before my parents and Conchita arrived, I moved out of the boarding house and into an apartment. Between the bond, the down payment for the apartment, and other expenses, I probably had $100 left to my name.

I would be leaving for my new position in the US in just a few weeks to train at Ronson, but Conchita would have to stay in Toronto with my parents.

Yet another complication was the fact that I would be leaving for my new position in the US in just a few weeks or months to train at Ronson while Conchita stayed in Toronto with my parents. Having just been granted permanent residence in Canada, she would now have to apply for a new visa to the United States and wait for approval. She was not pleased about that, nor was I—but what could we do?

After traveling from the Philippines to San Francisco and then Canada, via steamship and train the same way I had—a journey of three weeks (over far rougher seas than I'd experienced!)—Conchita arrived in Canada on July 24, 1959. We hadn't seen each other in two years. She was as beautiful as I remembered, all four foot ten of her. We got settled in the apartment and prepared for the wedding. We interviewed with the Catholic priest together and separately, and I suppose he found us compatible as the wedding was set for the next Saturday, the first of August. There was the question of who would walk Conchita down the aisle, since her family, sadly, wouldn't be there. Though my parents would attend, it didn't seem right for the father of the groom to escort the bride. Before I had moved to Canada, some friends in the Philippines had urged me to contact friends of theirs in Toronto, the Faulkners, an Englishman married to a Filipino woman. I had enjoyed having lunches and dinners with them over the months, so I asked Mr. Faulkner to walk Conchita down the aisle, and he obliged.

Also in attendance at the wedding, along with my parents, sister, and brothers, were a few former coworkers from Lucas Rotax and my former English landlady and her husband. I wore a dark suit, a white shirt, and a dark tie. Conchita wore a white lace, long-sleeved tea-length dress, pearls, and white heels, and she carried a spray of red roses and stephanotis. I had gone to Birks Jeweler's, a famous jewelry store in Toronto, and bought Conchita both an engagement ring and a wedding ring. The engagement ring was a little diamond, so small that you could hardly see it. I also bought a wedding band for myself. I'm quite sure I bought them on layaway, as I had no spare cash. Years later when we were comfortable financially, I bought Conchita a larger diamond ring (1.1 carat). She gave the little ring to our young daughter, who wore it for a while.

*I bought Conchita an engagement ring with
a little diamond so small that you could hardly see it.*

*Our wedding photo, 1959. A friend of ours offered
to take formal photo in his home, a few days after
(that is a fake bouquet).*

One of our friends filmed our wedding on his 8 mm camera,
but we had no formal photos. The wedding reception took place
in the middle of the afternoon in the basement event space of a
restaurant. At that time Canada was a dry country, so restaurants couldn't serve alcohol. The workaround was that people
would bring their own champagne or liquor and the restaurant
would provide soda or other mixers (whether that was within
the law or not, I'm not sure).

*Conchita and me on our honeymoon, 1959. We spent
a few nights in a hotel at Niagara Falls;
it was all we could afford!*

For our honeymoon we drove to Niagara Falls, about two hours away. I could only afford for us to stay in a motel for three or four nights. The rooms were little cabins scattered across the property, perfect for a new couple who wanted to be left alone. We then returned to our new apartment and my family in Toronto.

Less than a month after our honeymoon, I packed up my Zephyr and drove 1,200 miles from Toronto to Charlotte to start my new job at Ronson Hydraulics. I was driving on US highways for the first time.

*One of the reasons Conchita and I had such a successful
marriage was that she was an optimist as well and wanted
a life of adventure and challenge as much as I did.*

Though I had no job and little money when my fiancé and family arrived in Canada, I don't recall suffering or being worried or depressed. I was born with a certain sense of optimism, and I think it has served me well. The fact that I don't dwell on unpleasant events or hard times—whether personal, professional, or financial—has made me more confident and resourceful as an entrepreneur, because highs and lows are bound to happen. I tend to have a selective memory when it comes to my past and choose to dwell on the good times and seldom on the bad—and that has helped me to move forward. One reason Conchita and I had such a successful marriage was that she was an optimist as well and wanted a life of adventure and challenge as much as I did. We would need that optimism and resourcefulness to face certain challenges in the years ahead.

WHY AIRPLANE VALVES?

Working at Lucas Rotax strengthened my resolve to pursue a career in designing airplane valves. I credit that job for educating me about the use of valves on aircraft fuel control systems, and about the design of highly sophisticated fluid control valves. Learning to design a valve was not something a mechanical engineering student was taught in school. We learned the basic principles of hydraulics and pneumatics and laws of physics. We learned about strength and materials and thermodynamics and hydrodynamics. Applying that knowledge and information into designing hardware was the job, and I enjoyed it.

People might wonder how I could have spent an entire career designing airplane valves. I often wonder how people feel fulfilled making bagels all day long, for example. Or making pizzas. (Well, pizzas might be a little more interesting than bagels.) But airplane valves are nothing like pizza or bagels. They're complex, a real design puzzle. They continue to challenge and interest me to this day.

I find aircraft valve design very creative.
There are so many ways to arrive at a solution.

I find aircraft valve design very creative. There are so many ways to arrive at a solution. Building a valve using the fewest amount of parts improves the valve's reliability and may also lower the cost. So that's the challenge: designing the simplest solution for a highly sophisticated requirement. You might think that the more sophisticated the solution, the more expensive the valve, and that's often true. But the required reliability is the real reason airplane valves are so costly. The performance of an aircraft valve is critically important. It's not like a car or a lawn-mower—you can't say, "Well, I'm going to park in the sky and change this valve." You're in trouble if the valve fails. The plane will have to land immediately and have the valve replaced, or it's going to crash.

There are so many elements of valve design that made it a good business in the first place and continue to do so today. Patentability, however, is not one of them. Valve design is not usually patentable. Most of the concepts I use have been used many, many times by others in the field. The challenge is recon-ceiving and re-engineering these concepts into a more efficient package to make the product competitive.

There are many elements of valve design that made it a good business and continue to do so today.

I had been interested in airplanes since I was a boy, seeing them in the movies or in wartime propaganda films. I had pursued mathematics and science in high school in anticipation of studying engineering in college. During my college years, I would sometimes go to the Manila airport just to watch planes take off and land, or go to air shows put on by the US Air Force. I even brought Conchita on such excursions a few times; we we'd go to the airfields and walk around to look at the different models. I wanted her to understand my interest in airplanes.

I knew that the military and commercial aircraft industries were on the rise. Early airplanes used the internal combustion engine, which was noisy and created lots of vibration. But the gas turbine jet engine was becoming widely used and was changing the industry; it was quieter, had less vibration, and produced higher thrust. That's what had made it intriguing to me as an engineering student. I wrote my college thesis on gas turbine engines, and that had helped me get my job at Lucas Rotax.

During World War II, the US built most of the Allied airplanes because of its distance from Europe and Asia. There was less danger of the enemy coming to bomb the factories. America became the arsenal of democracy. Growing up in Shanghai and Manila, as I've said, we thought the streets of America were paved with gold. Of course, the US was known for automobile design, and many of the people who designed airplanes and engines around the world moved there as well. For example, I once visited the Sikorsky Aircraft headquarters in Connecticut and met this man in a baseball cap walking around the shop, chatting with people. The engineers said, "Hey, there's Igor Sikorsky." This pioneer of helicopter and fixed-wing design had immigrated from Russia to the United States in 1919. If you were interested in aircraft design, America was the place to be.

Without getting too technical, I will explain the process of designing a valve. First comes sizing the diameter of the valve. An aircraft manufacturer would say, for example, "I want a valve that can handle a hundred gallons per minute at a certain amount of pressure drop." My task was to determine if it was going to be a one-inch diameter or a ten-inch diameter valve, depending on the amount of fluid flow.

Once the diameter is determined, you must design the components that cause a valve to shut off, to open partially, or to be fully open. You might do this manually, using a knob—like a faucet on your sink—or electrically. I often use electricity to create an electromotive force that operates the valve, turning it fully open or fully closed.

You don't have to be knowledgeable about all the workings of an airplane to design a valve. The client provides the environment and constraints of the specific space. They might say, "The valve is going to be in a space equivalent to a four-inch cube."

They'll tell you what line sizes or tubing size is going into the valve; for example, "The line size is one-inch-diameter tubing." The internal valve cannot be any bigger than the tubing, so if it's a one-inch tube, the valve might be only three-quarters of an inch equivalent. The valve is designed to accommodate standard fittings, but the internal design of the valve is customizable.

You don't have to be knowledgeable about all
the workings of an airplane to design a valve.

These designs are not technically unique or patentable. There are probably other valves in the marketplace that look quite similar to what I've designed. But I have built into my design certain innovations that others don't have. If I can design an identically functioning valve with fewer parts, it's usually less complicated and therefore cheaper, and maybe even more reliable.

Usually my design involves the input of other engineers as well. A lot of information is exchanged back and forth as the product is improved, and at the end there could be a half-dozen people who have contributed to adjusting and refining a design. I enjoy the teamwork, for the most part. Sometimes it's difficult, and like everything else in life, you must compromise. Sometimes you may have to eat some humble pie and say, "Your design is better than mine. I'll adopt this feature that you're suggesting."

Aircraft valves have lots of special requirements. They are extremely customized, and the quantities produced are low. Probably only about 2,500 airplanes are built every year. The valves last millions of life cycles, or actuations. In aircraft, that is measured in flight time; It could be 30,000 or 50,000 hours of flight time before the valve needs to be replaced. As for materials, we usually use stainless steel and aluminum, but we also use exotic materials such as titanium, which can withstand higher temperatures.

Basically there are four types of valves: pressure or flow regulating valves, pressure check valves, solenoid electro-magnetic controlled valves, and servo (electrohydraulic) valves. As for designs, there are many—poppet valves, ball valves, slide valves, butterfly valves, gate valves, swinging check valves. These are names that try to illustrate the configuration; the swinging check valve is just like a door that opens and then closes automatically by a spring action. A single Boeing jet might use 100 valves of various sizes and functions.

The aircraft industry relies on experienced engineers. Companies will only place orders with people who have prior experience building a certain type of valve, so the longer you are in business, the better your chances of getting the job. In the industry, this is referred to as "pedigree." The client might say, "What is the pedigree on this design?" Then we'll explain, "This is a pedigree design from a Boeing 747 valve, with a slight modification. These are the additional improvements that we need to meet your requirements."

It's important to explain to your sales team what
the special features of your design are and
what is unique about your solution.

With enough pedigree, a sales team will be able to recommend your valve over someone else's. It's important to explain to the sales team just what the special features are and what's unique about your solution. The client might need some modifications or adjustment, so we go back and forth until finally it becomes a valve design that's acceptable to all the concerned parties. Often the issue is price, so we start looking to see how to make the part simpler and cheaper in order to compete.

Since the mid-1970s, designs have been drawn using CAD—computer-aided design. But back when I was in school we used translucent drafting paper. In my early years as an engineer, we'd use tracing paper or drafting paper on a drafting board, using a drafting machine. When drawings were completed they were printed with a blueprint machine and we'd send copies to different shops to see who could make the part most inexpensively. In fact, even the manufacturing itself was done with a manual machine. In the 1960s such machines cost maybe $10,000 to $15,000, and you might need ten machines to make a part. But now those machines are obsolete. Today's machine might cost $250,000, but it does things faster and more precisely.

After six decades in the business, a complex valve design is still a challenge I enjoy.

After six decades in the business, a complex valve design is still a challenge I enjoy. Even at the age of eighty-seven, I find myself staying up late at night working on designs. I feel fortunate to have found a career that has sustained me and my family for all these years.

CHARLOTTE, NORTH CAROLINA

After driving to Charlotte from Toronto, I rented a small one-bedroom duplex apartment on Margaret Wallace Road, basically out in the country. My first impression was that Charlotte was a small Southern town. Up until then I'd always lived in large metropolises—Shanghai, Manila, and Toronto. (Charlotte would eventually become one as well.) But at that time, everything in life felt like an adventure. I met the neighbors in the adjoining duplex, a young newly married couple named Knox and Norma Gardner, and they seemed friendly and welcoming.

Ronson Hydraulics made hydraulic controls for various military and commercial aircraft. My experience with valves at Lucas Rotax in Canada had gotten me the position. Ronson's Charlotte facility supported an important anti-aircraft missile program. The US was in the middle of the Cold War with Russia, and the government feared that Russia might fly over Canada to bomb the United States. They established a Distant Early Warning (DEW) line, an aerial defense line informed by radar stations across Canada. This system of radar stations, financed by both the US and Canada, was meant to defend the US or give the government early warning of any Russian aircraft coming from Siberia across the North Pole to the US. If an aircraft passed the DEW line, guided missiles or fighter aircrafts would be deployed to shoot it down.

This was a good job, and I was proud to be working on an important mission. I had first become interested in airplanes as a small boy watching Japanese propaganda newsreels during World War II in a Shanghai movie house, and now I was helping to build anti-aircraft missiles to shoot down the enemy. Of course, I was just providing little valves for one little subsystem, and I never even saw the full missile. In fact, those missiles were never deployed. But I was proud just the same. I always say to people that I was happy that none of my valves were ever operated in anger, because the stated goal of the mission was to destroy the missile or aircraft, in turn perhaps killing the crew.

I had first become interested in airplanes as a small boy watching Japanese propaganda newsreels during World War II in a Shanghai movie house, and now I was helping to build anti-aircraft missiles to shoot down the enemy.

Many antiwar people might have said at the time, and might say even now, "I'm not going to work for that company because it makes armaments to kill human beings." But I believe that the only way for a country to defend itself is to have strength. If you're strong as a country, the enemy is not going to threaten you. Such posturing between international powers still happens, and it will probably go on forever.

Ronson believed that their engineers should be good designers, as all designs began on paper. From there the designs moved to a drafting department. The parts were then detailed, and the designs were returned to engineering for any necessary adjustments or corrections. After that they were released to the manufacturing company, which would make the parts.

In Canada I hadn't done design work but mostly testing and control-valve performance analysis—and not with a computer, as they didn't yet exist, but with a slide rule, graphs, and charts. And I had only worked on fuel control valves for aircraft engines. But Ronson gave me the opportunity to not only design the valves but to work on all sorts of hydraulic controls. Though in my twenties I was eating, sleeping, and breathing airplane design, I took what was only my second airplane flight to travel to the Ronson Hydraulics headquarters in Pasadena, California, to learn how to be a design draftsman. I'd learned these skills in school but had never applied them. Now I had an opportunity to use my drafting skills to design products for manufacture. It was a big deal, and I was very excited.

I remember that when I began, I was extremely diligent. I'd come back into work at the company in the evenings, when the lighting wasn't the best. I'd work until my eyes were tearing from fatigue. The engineering group wasn't very big, only about six of us. I was the recruit. But after three months I was proficient on the drafting board. In fact, the first two valves I designed—pressure relief valves for the Nike Ajax missile—were approved by Douglas Aircraft and a purchase order was issued. It was a great win for the company, and I cherished my "beginner's luck"! Of course, the valves were designed with the help of other engineers. But basically they were my designs, and I continued enhancing them when I returned to Charlotte.

I had told Ronson that while working in Pasadena I would need a suite with a kitchen so that my wife could do some cooking. Once her papers were complete, Conchita joined me at the Rose Bowl Motel on Colorado Avenue, right by the Rose Bowl stadium. We always considered this time in Pasadena as our real honeymoon. After the wedding we'd only been able to afford a few nights at Niagara Falls. But this was a nice hotel, and other than my job we had no distractions and a few months on our own to get to know each other.

Conchita stayed at the hotel most of the day, watching TV, writing letters, and "cooking." To be honest, she wasn't really prepared to be a housewife. At home in the Philippines, her mother or a servant had done the cooking for the family. When she was in college she ate at the cafeteria. She had to learn how to cook from scratch, and she wasn't crazy about it. She didn't even know how to fry an egg, or cook bacon. When she tried to boil rice, it was too watery. I wasn't much help, as I didn't know how to cook much, either. But like all lovers, we lived on love and air.

Like all lovers, Conchita and I lived on love and air.

Conchita and I were young and enjoyed each other's company, and embarking on life together was an exhilarating experience for us. I was newly married, living in a new country with a new job, learning new skills. Conchita was excited as well. She'd seen Canada and was now living in the United States—and in California, where everyone wanted to go. Quite an adventure for a girl raised in the Philippines! Back in Toronto, my father found a job quite easily. Of course, my parents would have liked for us to stay in Canada, or to have joined us in the States, but they knew that this job at Ronson was a great opportunity for me. In Canada I had been making $5,000 Canadian dollars per year, but now my starting salary was $7,500 US (although at that time the Canadian dollar was worth more than the American dollar). Money was still tight, but I was able to catch up on my bills now that I again had a paycheck.

Besides my two designs becoming production items, there were other exciting events during our time in Pasadena. The first was that toward the end of our stay we took a trip to Disneyland in Anaheim, about an hour away. The "Happiest Place on Earth" had been founded in 1955, just five years before, and it was wildly popular. Everyone told us, "You *have* to go Disneyland before you go back to North Carolina!"

The other exciting development was that Conchita was feeling terrible—as she was pregnant. We had to stop several times on the way to Disneyland to allow her morning sickness to pass, and she couldn't do many of the rides. The only thing that Conchita could eat was grapefruit, which she was devouring like crazy. We didn't go to a doctor, but we knew she had to be pregnant.

When we left Pasadena and settled in Charlotte, that was also a happy time in our lives. I worked a lot but I enjoyed my job. I had a good salary. Our neighbors Knox and Norma became fast friends. We were constantly together, watching television in the evenings or occasionally dining at a nice restaurant. Knox was an accountant. I had only one week of vacation a year, other than the regular national holidays, but we did find time to go with the Gardners to Myrtle Beach, South Carolina, a popular seaside resort.

Norma was a Southern gal. She had never met an Asian person before and was intrigued by the differences in how we looked and talked, and by our backgrounds. She and Conchita became best buddies. In North Carolina, Conchita enjoyed her first snowfall. Norma had to teach her how to dress warmly. I had experienced winters in Shanghai and Canada, but it was all new for Conchita, and she loved it.

Asian people were not a common sight in the South at the time, but I didn't suffer any discrimination, at least not outwardly. Sadly, blacks were a different story; they were terribly discriminated against. They had to sit in the back of public buses and couldn't go to many restaurants, or if they could, they had to use a "black" bathroom. In the 1950s Charlotte became a center of civil rights protests and reform. Just a few years before I arrived, the city's African-American leaders had successfully desegregated Revolution Park.

I would go out for lunch most days with my boss, often to a Howard Johnson's to get a quick meal. In February of 1960, some 200 students from Johnson C. Smith University organized sit-ins at lunch counters across Charlotte, and there was a large demonstration outside ours. The police were there. As a result of these sit-ins, all lunch counters in the city were desegregated. Both in Canada and the United States, I think Asians escaped discrimination because we were offering specific skills for the most part and were not a threat to most people's jobs and livelihoods.

As happy as we were in Charlotte, Conchita and I also experienced our first tragedy there. We lost the baby, whom we had named Joseph. He was born prematurely, at only six months. His lungs were not fully developed, and in those days the only way to keep him alive was to put him in an incubator. But the doctor said if they gave him too much oxygen he would have brain damage. The incubator would possibly help him survive, but the doctor warned me ahead of time that Joseph would most likely not make it. Within ten hours the baby passed away. We buried him in a cemetery in Charlotte.

When Conchita went into labor early, we didn't even think about Joseph not making it. We were young and ignorant, and the gravity of his condition came as a total shock. We were distraught, but we didn't feel that we were deficient in any way physically. It had simply been that the child was born prematurely, and at the time medical options weren't available. After about a year we began to try again to have a baby. We were surprised that Conchita became pregnant quite quickly. We still mourned Joseph and were nervous about the pregnancy and delivery, but when Patricia was born on July 3, 1961, safe and healthy at nine months, we were overjoyed. Our joy was amplified as our friend Norma was also pregnant, and she had a baby girl as well.

Patricia was a good baby. We even took her on a trip to Asheville, in the mountains of North Carolina. We had a little crib that hung over the backs of the front seats. Patricia was a great traveler. Once we put her into that bed, the car lulled her to sleep.

After four years in Charlotte, I received an interesting phone call from an executive at United Aircraft Products in Dayton, Ohio. United didn't make valves; they made heat exchangers for aircraft. Picture an old-fashioned steam radiator—it was the same concept. I wasn't interested in heat exchangers, but United was looking to broaden their base. They wanted to create a whole new division to manufacture valves and were looking to hire a seasoned valve engineer.

I thought about the opportunity. It was a better paying position. We were starting to feel very far from my family in Toronto, and we wanted to be a little closer. Ohio wasn't close, but it was only about half as far as Charlotte. My parents hadn't even been to visit us in Charlotte; my father was working in the offices at Canadian Institute of the Blind. My brother was still working in Sarnia, and my sister had become a teacher in Canada. We spoke on the phone, but in those days long-distance calls were expensive, so we only really talked on holidays or birthdays. We had moved from the duplex into a bigger house, on Dresden Drive closer to downtown Charlotte, where we were still renting. Knox and Norma had moved as well, and we still saw them a lot but not as often as before. I was close to my boss, Richard Fuller, general manager at Ronson. He was a former submarine officer and had been a good mentor. Conchita and I had become friendly with him and his wife, Mary. He was disappointed that I was leaving the company, but when I told him why, he understood.

Now I was making decisions not just for myself, but for Conchita and my little daughter Patricia.

It was time to take the next step on my adventure. I accepted the job in Dayton and was excited to create this new division.

Of course, now I was making decisions not just for myself but also for Conchita and my little daughter Patricia. And, as often happens in life, things did not go quite as planned.

DAYTON, OHIO

When you're young and naive, things often seem easier than when you know too much. In 1962 Conchita and I packed up our blue American Motors Rambler station wagon (I had traded in my Ford Zephyr for a "family car") and bundled up one-year-old Patricia to head to my new job at United Aircraft Products in Dayton. We rented an apartment in a brand-new, two-story building without thinking too much about it. Our spirit of adventure endured.

When you're young and naive, things often seem easier than when you know too much.

That Monday I reported to work at United Aircraft and went to see the man who had hired me. But when I got to his office, another man was sitting there. He said, "Oh, he's no longer with the company." He had been fired!

Fortunately, his replacement didn't dismiss me. "We don't know what to do with you," he said. "But since my predecessor hired you, we will honor our obligation." I was relieved. The company was going to proceed with creating the valve division that I'd been hired to launch. He could easily have told me to turn around and go back to Charlotte!

Back at our new apartment, Conchita met a woman named Hope Footer. Hope and her husband, Larry, were a young couple like us, and they had also recently moved to town. Much like Norma and Knox Gardner in Charlotte, they became two of our closest friends. They lived on the upper floor, while we were on the ground floor. We were still like kids at that time; we'd go swimming in the community pool, have picnics, watch football. Hope and Conchita confided in each other and talked about *everything*. Let's just say that after their conversations, Hope at long last was able to get pregnant!

Our time in Dayton marked the first time my parents came to visit us in the States. They were now able to travel freely, having become Canadian citizens. When our second child, a son we named Michael Paul, was born on February 2, 1965, at Good Samaritan Hospital, my mother came to help after Conchita returned home. Patricia was now a toddler—and a handful. It was a bit stressful for my mother, as she hadn't taken care of a baby in nearly thirty years (and had had a servant at the time!). She stayed for a week or two to help us get back on our feet.

Dayton was a boomtown in the 1960s, its population at its all-time peak. It had become a manufacturing center during World War II, and after the war veterans and others flocked to the area in search of jobs. The city sprawled into suburbs, and more than 100,000 homes were built in the 1950s to house the influx of residents. After the war, United Aircraft specialized in designing and manufacturing aircraft heat exchanges, which were in high demand.

But as quickly as we had arrived in Dayton, our time there came to an end. Soon after arriving at United Aircraft, I started designing valves as planned. I sent the designs to the company's contacts in the aircraft industry and pushed hard to sell them for about a year. But at the end of that time we hadn't gotten a single contract. It turned out that aircraft companies didn't want valves designed by a company known for heat exchangers, especially from a new division. My team couldn't quote the valves competitively, mainly because they didn't have the manufacturing expertise. I knew how to design the valves, but when I gave the fabrication team the drawings they didn't know how to make them efficiently and cost-effectively. As a result our prices were always too high, so we couldn't compete. And I sensed that rectifying the situation was not a priority for United Aircraft.

Though my firing may have been imminent, I was the one to approach the company management. "I'm sorry," I said. "I'm quitting. I can't accept being in the position of proposing all these designs and nothing happening." They completely understood, and I left on good terms.

It was a hard decision, but in truth I was already working on a Plan B. I had been approached by Drew Morris of GW Lisk about a position. In Charlotte, when working for Ronson Hydraulic, I had bought solenoids from him, as we didn't manufacture them. When he saw me move to a job in Dayton, he called on me, trying to sell me the same products—and to sell me on a job at his own company. I think he sensed that things weren't going well at United Aircraft.

Drew said to me, "Confidentially, if you're unhappy with this job, I have an offer for you. If you're willing to move to Clifton Springs, New York—which is much closer to your family in Toronto—I know of a company that might hire you." He had partnered up with a valve manufacturer called Wright Components, whose founder was Bill Wright, and the company was proving to be quite successful. It was a small company, and Drew and Bill were co-owners and salesmen. All they were missing was a chief engineer to head up the program.

I looked up Clifton Springs on the map. A small town with a population of about 2,000, it was situated between Rochester and Syracuse—about three-and-a-half hours by car from Toronto. Its proximity to the Rochester Institute of Technology and other universities made it relatively easy to hire engineers. This was going to be my fourth job, and I was just thirty years old. But it wasn't unusual for engineers to change jobs in those days; often they would move from one company to another until they found their ideal situation.

This was going to be my fourth job,
and I was just thirty years old.

Though Conchita was now the mother of two small children and had made good friends in Dayton, she wasn't upset about moving. We hadn't seen much of each other since we'd moved to Dayton about a year before. I had spent many long hours at United Aircraft trying to drum up business for my division—remember, there were no computers, and I didn't have a drafting board at home. That meant lengthy days at the office. Conchita understood but at the same time was somewhat disturbed that I was spending so much time at work.

It wasn't a difficult move. All our belongings fit into one little moving van. We packed up the station wagon again—this time with two kids—and drove seven hours to Clifton Springs.

CLIFTON SPRINGS, NEW YORK

The last time I'd been in upstate New York was on our honeymoon to Niagara Falls—which was actually not far from Clifton Springs. Over the coming years we'd visit Niagara Falls as often as we could. Clifton Springs was indeed a small town, much smaller than anywhere we had lived before. When we built a house a few years later, our mailing address was simply "Cruz, East Main Street." At the time there were fewer than ten houses on our street, surrounded by fields. People would say, "That's the Cruz residence" or "That's the Kahn residence." The postman knew where it was.

In the 1960s Clifton Springs was basically a small town of hardworking people involved in manufacturing. Wright Components was one of the few small manufacturing companies in town. I became its chief engineer for the company. Bill Wright, my boss, had been involved in valve manufacturing and testing for another company before this one, but he didn't have an engineering degree. Drew Morris, financier for Wright Components, provided Bill with most of the money to start the business, so Drew owned most of the stock. I also met an engineer named Ray Ganowsky, who'd a been hired by Drew to start a rotary solenoid division called Cliftronic Co. He arrived in Clifton Springs at about the same time that I did, and we became lifelong friends. Our intrepid department secretary was Eileen Ciardi.

The aircraft industry at the time had some ups and downs but was basically stable. The company campus was a complex of homes that had been converted into offices. I was starting up the airplane valve division, so I had to hire all the other engineers. Rochester was the nearest big city, home to not only the

Rochester Institute of Technology but also the University of Rochester and Ryerson University; the University of Buffalo was nearby. Luring engineers to a small town like Clifton Springs was a challenge, but the location was attractive to engineers who preferred to live out in the country, so to speak. Many of them were willing to sacrifice a higher salary for the sake of improved living conditions.

In the early years Bill Wright and I had a very good relationship. I was able to handle most of the technical issues, and Bill was a good salesman. When we went on the road to pitch our services to clients, I would explain the technical aspects and he would seal the deal. Bill was very outgoing. On road trips, every night he'd say, "Okay, Paul. Let's go to the bars." In those days the favorite bars for men on business expense accounts were the go-go joints where girls clad in skimpy clothing danced on a stage or on the bar. I'm not going to say I didn't enjoy it, but Bill was at another level altogether. He'd be drinking most of the time, more than seemed healthy.

I'll never forget one business trip to Cincinnati, Ohio. My travel partner was not Bill but John, another salesman at the company, along with another guy who loved to drink and hit the nightspots. It was part of the job: we'd invite clients out, and it was almost required that we show them "a good time." On this night we had an important client—General Electric's large engine division. With the GE team we hopped from one bar to another, and then another. By midnight I said to John, "We'd better get back to the hotel," and we hopped into his car.

The hotel had a multistory parking lot. As the car wound its way up the circular ramp, I started feeling worse and worse. When we parked, I got out and threw up. I was embarrassed, but John was laughing his head off. "Oh well, you'll be okay," he said. "You'll sleep well tonight." When we parted company at our rooms, we said, "Let's make sure we get going by 8 am."

We had a meeting at 9 am with the same people we'd just been entertaining. So I got up at 8 am and took a quick shower, then prettied myself up a bit. I called John and asked, "Ready?"

"No," he said, "not yet."

I said, "What's wrong with you?"

"I can't get out of bed!" he said. "You did the right thing by throwing up."

By the time we got to GE we were late, and the purchasing manager said, "What happened, John?" And John said, "Well, I wasn't feeling well this morning." The guy laughed. "I certainly know why!" But at the end of the day, we got the order from them.

The company salesmen traveled often, but I'd only go on the road every other month or so. I enjoyed it, but my trips were for just two or three days. If we were in California, for example, the salesman and I would visit a few clients. But after I went home, the salesman would stay the rest of the week and try to contact other companies in the area. I had kids and a wife to attend to, and it was always great to come home and be reunited with them.

In today's modern business climate, business entertaining isn't go-go bars and expense accounts. If anything, we'll have lunch catered at the office before a meeting with a client, and if we go out to dinner, everyone pays their own way. Everything is much stricter, and the business environment is better and more ethical as a result.

On that Cincinnati business trip I learned a valuable lesson about maintaining control. Ever since then I've never over-imbibed, because I learned from that experience when to stop drinking. If I had a drink, it would be one scotch on the rocks. These days I barely drink at all—I have no attachment to liquor. I probably have a cocktail once every two weeks.

I learned a valuable lesson on that business trip about maintaining control.

Unfortunately, there were dark clouds forming. Bill's drinking began to affect the business. When he started missing work, Drew said, "I have to get involved." Eventually he felt he had to fire Bill. Bill's wife left him and he went back to live with his parents; he died in his parents' home, long before his time. It was tragic. His parents had been so proud of him when we started the business. I remember that when I first joined him and the company, he had bought his father a new car. After Bill left the company, he would visit us occasionally. But sadly, he died with nothing.

Drew had bought out Bill's shares in the company, which left Drew as sole owner. He hired another general manager for Wright Components, to whom I reported. But as chief engineer I worked pretty much unencumbered, and we got along well.

When we moved to Clifton Springs, we once again rented an apartment. But after a few years we bought an acre-and-a-half tract of land and built a house. We bought the property from Jane and Joe Kahn, who had a big plot of land on which sharecroppers planted corn during the summer months, but Joe had decided he wanted to sell some of it for homes. The house we built was small, maybe about 1,500 square feet. At that time it was big enough for us, since the kids were still small. It wasn't a spectacular house; in fact, it was very simple, a three-bedroom house with two baths. The lot was quite large, and we had to maintain the grass, so we ended up buying a Sears riding lawn mower. Conchita learned how to drive it and enjoyed that, so she ended up taking care of the lawn, riding the mower up and down the property. Of course, we only cut the grass a few months of the year in upstate New York. The rest of the year it was cold and snowy!

Clifton Springs was the quintessential small town. There may have been a movie house, but if so, I don't remember it! People were very involved in family life, with Little League and kids' sports. Bowling was a popular activity, because in the long winter you couldn't do much outdoors. We'd bowl, have drinks, and socialize. People would have house parties as well. We had lots of friends.

What I remember from Clifton Springs and my thirties is work, work, and more work. On a typical day I'd work at the office from 9 am to 5 pm, but very often I'd do quite a bit of drafting at home as well. At that time there were no portable computers. All calculations were done with a log-log slide rule. When the kids were little, Conchita was a full-time mother, but once they started going to school she found a part-time job. She worked for Clifton Springs Hospital as a clerk handling orders for the pharmacy. She was happy being busy and earning a few extra bucks. Conchita always liked to work.

> *What I remember from Clifton Springs and my thirties is work, work, and more work.*

I became a member of the Rotary Club. Being new in town, that was a good way to meet other businesspeople: doctors, lawyers, salesmen. We met every week in a local restaurant, and I was made president of the Rotary in 1974. I didn't find much professional benefit to it, but it was a good social gathering.

Church was another big weekend activity, as in most small towns. We met a lot of people through church, and I was even a Sunday school teacher for a while. I joked with the priest, saying, "You know, I'm not a very religious person. You sure I qualify?" He said, "Sure. As long as you're somewhat knowledgeable about the Bible." He provided me with enough instructional material that I could at least explain some of the catechism to the children. Anyway, the kids were so young that they weren't that interested, and I spent more time quieting them down than teaching them! I didn't really enjoy it. Years later when I visited Clifton Springs, a young man came up to me and said, "You used to be my Sunday school teacher." I didn't remember him, but of course he wasn't a kid anymore!

As for my own children, we now had three: Patricia, Michael, and Steven, who was born in December of 1967. Clifton Springs was a great place for them to grow up. There was no crime to speak of, so the kids had a lot of freedom. They had lots of friends, played sports, and took the school bus every morning. On weekends we'd play board games—Monopoly, chess, checkers. And we'd play sports out on our big lawn. There was a rock pile with garden snakes in it, so we'd go watch them squirm around. Every once in a while you'd see a deer running through the cornfield. When the corn got tall, the kids would wander into the cornfield, way to the far end of the property. They liked to climb the big oak tree that stood right in the middle of the farm. We'd also watch television together (a color TV was a big improvement).

Clifton Springs was a great place for the children to grow up.

As for vacations, we were certainly not well-off enough for elaborate trips, but we often visited Toronto. We'd stay in my parents' apartment and enjoy the larger city's wealth of activities—zoos, movie houses, restaurants. In fact, many of our friends from the United States would meet us in Canada. One of Conchita's sisters had moved to Canada as well—her only sibling to leave the Philippines. Sometimes we'd take the train down to New York City, which we enjoyed.

One major event during our years in Clifton Springs was that Conchita and I became US citizens. We had become very friendly with our next-door neighbors, the Kahns, from whom we'd bought our land. I had my green card, which meant I was a permanent resident and paid taxes. But since I was quite politically conscious, I wanted to be able to vote. In Canada I'd been able to vote, as I was a British citizen—and that was the last time I had voted.

I applied to become a US citizen and asked the Kahns if they would be our sponsors. I don't remember much about the process, but there were a lot of forms to fill out, and I had to take a written test on American history. Without too much difficulty, Conchita and I became citizens—and I voted in a presidential election for the first time. Like many immigrants, I registered as a Democrat, the party of John F. Kennedy and Robert F. Kennedy, whom I admired. I planned to vote in the 1968 for Bobby Kennedy, until he was assassinated in June of 1968. I believe I voted for Richard Nixon, the Republican candidate, but I remained a Democrat for years. At first glance the Democratic party appears to help immigrants much more than the Republican platform does. But as I grew older I leaned more Republican, though I didn't officially switch parties until 2016.

Another consequence of becoming a US citizen was that I had to report to Selective Service and register for the draft. The Vietnam War was simmering and about to boil over. As I was already in my thirties, I didn't expect that I'd be drafted if there was a call, so when I went to the Selective Service office I wasn't that concerned. The officer said, "I'm going to put you down as 4F." I asked, "What does that mean?" He told me, "It just means that you are married and have children and will probably not be drafted." (The actual definition is "found not qualified for service in the Armed Forces by a Military Entrance Processing Station under the established physical, mental, or moral standards"—in other words, I had been rejected!) At that time there was no draft. When the war wore on and the draft was instated, I wasn't called. Even if I had been, I was building valves for the war effort, so it was unlikely that I would have been eligible.

Though I was Asian, I felt that America's actions in the Vietnam War were correct. But when I talked to other Asians, they would say that wasn't true. Today I work with a Vietnamese chief designer at Valve Research, and he calls it the American War. He was a young child at the time. I followed the Vietnam War carefully but was fortunate not to know anyone who died. I knew that a lot of the valves I built were for Huey helicopters being shipped to Vietnam, first for medevac and then for expanded missions, as well for guided Shrike anti-radar missiles and Paveway laser-guided bombs. If that can be considered aiding the cause, I hope that's what I did.

I began to invest in the stock market when we were living in Clifton Springs. For the first time Conchita and I had a little extra money to play with, so when a group of people at the office started a stock investment club, I joined. It was called the CS (Clifton Springs) Speculators. We each chipped in $15 a month, and we used the funds to buy stocks. I thought, "What's $15? That's pocket money. I can lose it and I won't even care." I stayed a member for the nine years that I was in Clifton Springs, and even after we moved, because I liked the investment. But about five years after I left, the CS Speculators decided to call it quits, as many of the members were beginning to retire. We ended up selling off the stocks, and members used their profits to invest privately.

I loved being a CS Speculator, and it was a great introduction to investing. I applied what I learned to my own investments, but I was still young and ambitious and impatient, and I invested in cheaper stocks that were very risky, with little luck. In Clifton Springs I made little money in terms of my income, relatively speaking, and I made little money in terms of investments. The real investment was our home, which we bought for about $21,000.

Yes, money was always a big issue—in that I wasn't earning very much. My income was $25,000 a year, which was pretty good money in Clifton Springs! We were considered some of the richer people in town. In fact, our friends kidded us because we lived on "Mortgage Row," so nicknamed because all the new homeowners on the street had mortgages. As for the rest of the town, they lived in older homes and their mortgages had been paid off years ago.

Money was a big issue—in that I wasn't earning very much.

I enjoyed my work at Wright Components, but it didn't escape me that Drew Morris was getting richer and richer but I wasn't. His own company, which made solenoids, was doing well. Then he had Wright Components, which was also successful. He was making a lot of money, while my income pretty much stayed where it was. That income was satisfactory, but I began to think about how what I would be able to earn if I stayed in this job. Drew invited us to his fabulous home, full of beautiful furnishings and art. I said to myself, "Every one of these things is tied in with the number of solenoids he sells." He was able to acquire all this wealth because he had a product.

I returned to my father's words to me when I was a child: that it was better to own your own company than to make money for someone else.

The idea of starting my own business started to consume me. I thought, "Well, if there's no room for advancement here, I'll just go out and make my own products and make my own millions." I returned to my father's words to me when I was a child: that it was better to own your own company than to make money for someone else. They were truly words of wisdom. Ever since building that crystal radio set, I had wanted to manufacture and sell products. It had been a very small idea, but over time the notion had grown bigger.

There was another impetus for moving. Our daughter Patricia became terribly ill with allergies every spring, often having trouble breathing, and that was scary. It began as hay fever and eventually turned into asthma. We brought her to an allergist, and she was diagnosed with numerous allergies. At first we thought that she'd just have to live with it. But Patricia was in her early teens at that time, and she was becoming barrel-chested because of her asthma. Her ribs spread out a bit, and that was alarming. The doctor said, "That's common for people with asthma or allergies. She'll outgrow it." But we were concerned.

However, we discovered that when we were on vacation in Florida, where we'd travel for about a week every year, Patricia's asthma would disappear. We spoke to the allergist when we got back and found that her allergy to ragweed was related to where we lived. He told us, "You could move, but there are not very many places that don't have ragweed. Basically you can go to the desert of California or Arizona, or you could go to Florida." I was already thinking about moving to start my own business, so I thought, "I'd rather be in Florida, it's not as hot and dry." The tropical climate of Florida felt more familiar to me, having lived in Manila.

While the quest to start my own business was my biggest motivation to move, I really did feel that I needed to improve conditions for my daughter's health. And in fact, when we moved to Florida with Patricia's bagful of medications, we hurried to store them properly in the refrigerator. But after six months she'd never used any of them. We called the doctor in New York, who told us, "You're lucky. If I were you, I'd just throw it all away." So we—happily—tossed hundreds of dollars of medications into the trash.

The quest to start my own business was the biggest motivation to move to Florida, but I also needed to improve conditions for my daughter's health.

The move was well worth it. Patricia still occasionally has allergy flareups, but it is not an understatement to say that the move to Florida changed her life.

In 1969 we returned to the Philippines for a visit. It had been twelve years since I had gotten on a steamship and departed for my adventure in the Western world. Conchita had gone back to visit her family once when Patricia was about two years old. She had intended to stay for a few months, but the mosquitoes had been so bad—window screens weren't common—and Patricia had gotten so covered in bites that they came home after only a week or two.

Conchita and I returned to the Philippines in 1959.
We visited University of The Philippines, her alma mater.

Though my first trip back to the Philippines is now more than fifty years ago, I remember it well. We returned to our neighborhood in Manila, toured the city and all the old haunts. We visited with Conchita's family, whom I'd not seen in twelve years and who had never met Michael or Steven. I reflected that there had been slight improvements in daily life there, but people were still very distressed financially. I was no longer used to this type of environment.

I reflected that in Manila there had been slight improvements in daily life there, but the people were still very distressed financially.

In Manila I had never lived in a very poor area. Though my parents didn't have much money, we were still considered middle class. But a decade later, middle-class life in the Philippines seemed lower-class as compared to life in the United States. If my father had remained there, he would have struggled money-wise. In Canada he'd been able to get a good job at the Canadian Institute for the Blind, and my parents' financial situation was stable.

If I had stayed in the Philippines, I probably wouldn't have had the job opportunities that I'd had in the United States and Canada, because my family wasn't wealthy or connected. Even though I did have some upper-class friends there, their families tended to look out for their own. These were large families, with four or five or six kids, and any career opportunities were extended to them first. The only way I could have benefited was to have married into such a family.

I visited with some of my old classmates and college friends. I suppose their situations had improved a bit in the decade since I had left. But they had no dreams of leaving the country, with their families and jobs there. One of my old friends, an engineer, was married to my brother John's former girlfriend, whom he had left behind when he and I got on that steamship to America. In hindsight he probably should have married her, as she was a nice girl and came from a wealthy family that exported Philippine mahogany. When we first moved to Clifton Springs, Conchita and I had traveled to Buffalo to celebrate John's marriage to a woman he had met in Sarnia, a Belgian Canadian local. Over the years his work as an engineer had taken him to Mexico, Japan, and other countries. His wife had come along, but their marriage wasn't happy. She was a high-school dropout and didn't encourage their children to be serious students, which was unfortunate. They eventually divorced.

My brother Joe had been more successful in marriage. A chemical engineer, he lived in British Columbia, and was married, with three kids who ultimately became very successful as well. My sister Olivia was a teacher and librarian and lived in different cities around Canada. She never married, but in later years she was a great companion to my mother.

I didn't return to the Philippines again for many years. Conchita missed her family and traveled back to visit them on a few occasions, but she felt her life was in the United States. On one trip she took Patricia, then about ten years old, and for fun also took the Kahns' daughter, Barbie, who was a teenager. Patricia was very close to her cousins in the Philippines, more so than our other kids. But during those years I was more concerned with looking to the future than looking back, as I pondered the next steps in my career and my life.

I became more and more convinced that it was time to make a change, both professionally and personally. My father's advice drummed a steady beat in my thoughts—that it was better to make money for yourself than for someone else. It struck me that when I was thirty years old, I had had $10,000 in savings; I was now forty and *still* had $10,000 in savings. In the nine years we had lived in Clifton Springs, my salary had increased only incrementally, while Wright Components had enjoyed great success. In fact, Drew Morris—my boss, friend, and mentor—was now so wealthy that he decided to move back to his home state of California. His absence weighed on my mind. There was also Patricia's health condition. And frankly, I was fed up with the New York winters!

I became more and more convinced that it was time
to make a change, both professionally and personally.

Sadly my father did not live long enough to see me take his advice. In 1972 he died at the age of sixty-three. He had been a lifelong smoker. I remember that when I was little his fingers would be stained brown; his teeth and even his pillow were brown, and there was always ash everywhere. Growing up, I was more turned off by smoking being such a dirty habit than by the fear of cancer. In the Philippines everyone smoked, but as the windows were always open to let the breezes through, second-hand smoke was less of a health issue.

Eventually my father died of heart failure related to emphysema, which he struggled with for years. We buried him at a cemetery in Toronto, per his wishes. After his death we visited my mother more often, to help take her mind off her loss. As compared to my father's premature death, my mother lived another thirty years!

My father's death was a further reminder that life is short—there was no time to waste if we intended to change our circumstances. We put our house on the market and I let Wright Components know that it was my intention to leave.

It took about six months to sell our Clifton Springs house on Mortgage Row. I had bought the home and land for $21,000, and we sold it for $39,000. Once I paid off the mortgage, it wasn't a huge windfall. I had some investments. They weren't much, but I was looking at businesses that cost about $50,000, and my investments would allow me to pay for most of it—and, Conchita hoped, maybe even get a mortgage on a house.

I joked to my friends that I had three options for my midlife crisis: a new wife, climbing Everest, or starting my own business! I had no interest in the first two, so I went with the third—but I had no idea how to proceed. I knew I would need a manufacturing facility to build my products. And I thought if I purchased an existing machine shop, whatever it made, the revenue would allow me to get the valve manufacturing business off the ground. So I contacted a business broker, who was very helpful. He'd present me with information and financial statements from machine shops for sale around the country. Only one problem: I had no idea how to evaluate these statements.

> *I joked to my friends that I had three options for*
> *my midlife crisis: a new wife, climbing Everest,*
> *or starting my own business!*

So that's when I asked Knox Gardner, my friend and neighbor from our days in Charlotte, to help me. He was an accountant and could evaluate which businesses were financially stable. I'd send him the financial reports, and he would tell me, "This one's good" or "This one's no good." Most of these companies were going out of business.

Ultimately we found an operation in Florida that was still in business and whose financial situation was just barely acceptable to Knox. It was a machine shop called Jet Research in Fort Lauderdale. Knox said, "You could buy this one. It's doing okay, but it's on the rocks." At the time the business was focused mainly on making machine parts for Pratt & Whitney jet engines. I flew down to look at the facility, and Knox came along. It didn't look like much. Located at 999 Northwest 53rd Street in Fort Lauderdale, the building was only about 900 square feet.

Most of the manufacturing equipment looked old; everything was manually operated at the time. The owners said they would remain involved, and there were a few employees: two machinists and a salesman. It wasn't much, but it wasn't out of business!

I decided to make an offer. Knox negotiated the price to approximately $55,000. Using the proceeds from the sale of the house and my investments from being a CS Speculator, I paid mostly cash. I will never forget the date of the closing: October 21, 1974. I will also never forget the IRS agent who waiting outside the office as we signed the papers! The seller owed unpaid Social Security taxes, and if the business hadn't been sold he would have been arrested for nonpayment. I wrote one check to the IRS, one for commission to the business broker, and one for the remainder to the seller. I changed the name of the business to Valve Research and Manufacturing.

I was so grateful to Knox for helping me through this process. I said, "I don't have any money to pay you for your efforts, but I'm going to give you one share of the business." He protested, saying, "No, you don't have to give me part of the business—I did it as a friend." I insisted, "It's not much of an offer! My business might not succeed, and one share would mean nothing. But maybe someday it *will* be worth something." I drew up the shareholder letter. Knox grudgingly accepted it and tucked it away in a folder.

> *I insisted, "It's not much of an offer! My business might not succeed, and one share would mean nothing. But maybe someday it will be worth something."*

It was 1974. I was forty years old. I hadn't evaluated the labor market in South Florida, or the manufacturing landscape, or home prices, or anything else. I had no business plan. Basically I was flying blind. Thanks to my "midlife crisis," I was shedding my safe existence in New York and putting not only my future but that of my wife and three children at risk. But fortunately Conchita was supportive of this ambitious new plan. She had always shared my appetite for adventure.

One memorable night in Clifton Springs, Conchita and I pulled out our stack of airmail letters from before we were married, when I had traveled by steamship to Canada and she was still in the Philippines. They were aerogrammes on paper so thin that the fountain pen ink had bled through. Both my writing and hers weren't great, and over time the ink had gotten fainter and harder to read. They were the silly scrawls of young lovers that now seemed embarrassing! We thought, "What if the kids find these? Maybe we should just have a letter-burning ceremony." And so we did.

When the kids were in bed, we poured some wine and read through the dozens of letters, then threw them into the roaring fireplace. We giggled and said, "Did we say that? Did you say that?" It seemed like these letters had been written a lifetime ago. So many dreams and plans. Over the years we had made many of these dreams and plans come true! Sometimes I wish I still had those letters, silly as they were.

One of my childhood dreams had been to own my own business, and now here we were, about to make that dream come true. We once again packed up the family car. Off to Florida!

FLORIDA: THE EARLY YEARS, 1974–1979

Sometimes I wonder if being an entrepreneur is in my genes. But the truth is that my parents were very concerned about my entrepreneurial venture. Though my father had always encouraged me to "make money for myself instead of someone else," when it came to providing for his own grandchildren he felt differently! He and my mother were worried about whether I had prepared for the kids' educations, college tuition, and so on. I had to admit that I hadn't. I'd plowed all my savings into purchasing the business.

And while many people dream of starting their own businesses, leaving comfortable lives to shoot for the stars, most don't actually end up doing it. They don't want to be uprooted from their current environment. In Clifton Springs people would say, "I like my friends and neighbors here. If we move, we'll have to make new friends." Conchita and I didn't feel that way. We thought, "If we can improve ourselves, let's do it." We never had trouble finding friends, Conchita especially. She got to know people quickly, and before you knew it they were great friends. When she died, many people were distressed—they all felt that they had lost their best friend.

While many people dream of starting their own business, leaving their comfortable lives to shoot for the stars, most don't end up doing it.

Perhaps we had moved more times than most people. But the aircraft industry was especially transitory. Engineers would work for Northrop, and then when their contract was over they would simply go to another company that built the same type of airplane and was looking for engineers. Most of my friends in the aerospace industry have changed jobs at least ten times.

But I was not someone who liked to keep job-hopping for the prospect of a little more money. Engineers I knew would work on aircraft, then on automotives, or shipbuilding. I preferred to stick to the core product that I was interested in. I thought that valve design was a truly interesting field.

I may not have been handed down entrepreneurial genes, but I do think an appetite for risk ran in my family, and that served me well in business. When I began investing in the stock market in Clifton Springs, I realized that I liked to make money from owning something, whether it was stocks or a business. Home ownership and salary increases were too incremental! I felt that I'd have more control over a business than over the stock market. You had to accept the vagrancies of the market—up one day and down one day. You might have to sell a stock at a loss or buy it at an excessive price. But if you bought a business, you might at least have some kind of control—even though I had no idea how to run a business. I was a financially ignorant person. All I knew is that when I visited my boss Drew Morris's gorgeous house, it hit me that everything in it was tied to the number of solenoids he sold. He was able to acquire all that wealth just because he had a product.

> *I think an appetite for risk ran in my family.*
> *And that served me well in business.*

My brother John also thought I was crazy. But today he says, "I worked for all of these chemical companies, and I always thought about doing what you did, but I just didn't have the guts to go into it. I just didn't have the willpower." He had invented many chemicals that were patented, but the patents were all owned by the company. If he had quit the company and applied for patents independently, he could have hit it big. But he didn't have the desire to go into a venture that was somewhat risky.

I also had another asset that many men didn't have: an understanding wife. I think Conchita had confidence that I would make out okay. And as a business graduate herself from the University of Philippines, she knew that entrepreneurs had created great industries because they were willing to invest. Of course, that doesn't mean that in those early days of Valve Research she didn't have her own doubts!

After living in four countries and several cities, Florida became my permanent home. But my life of adventure was certainly not over. Building my own business took more twists and turns and caused more highs and lows than any relocation ever did.

To be honest, I knew a lot about valves but next to nothing about running a company. I had to learn from scratch. It was fortunate that I started by buying a machine shop, because that way I got to learn some of the manufacturing end of engineering. As a designer, of course I knew what a lathe was and what the Bridgeport milling machine was, and what they did. But as to how to estimate the cost of manufacturing machine parts with them? I had no idea.

I knew a lot about valves but next to nothing about running a company.

When I purchased the machine shop, I thought that being a service provider would generate revenue and provide a decent livelihood. In the meantime, I could take my time looking for customers for my valves. But running a machine shop turned out to be harder than it looked.

The manufacturing area in the Military Trail location, mid 1980s. We moved the manual machines from our first location; computer-operated machines did not exist yet.

The machine shop I purchased was contracted by large aircraft companies to manufacture a variety of parts, fittings, and tools that they didn't make themselves. These potential clients would send us the blueprints of parts and ask for estimates. Putting together an estimate was complex—and often I found myself flying blind on the costs! I would ask one machinist, "How much time do you think it will take you to make this part?" He would say five hours. But another machinist would tell me two hours. I was guessing, and out of my comfort zone—and for me it wasn't interesting or lucrative to just make other companies' parts. I was a designer, after all.

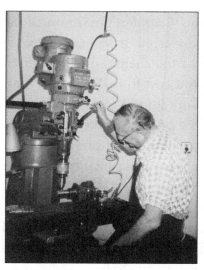

*A machinist at a Bridgeport mill
that is manually operated.*

In our original machine shop, c. 1975.

I realized that most machine shops are run by people who might be good machinists but were poor businessmen. How did this affect me? I would be underbid by competing machine shops all the time. Sometimes I'd win, sometimes I'd lose. But the ones that I won, I wouldn't make much money on. I would realize that I had underbid. It was a cutthroat business! And the worst part was that the clients—the aircraft companies—knew exactly how much it cost to make a part. That's why they were bidding out the work; they'd tried to make the part themselves and found that they couldn't make it for the price they wanted. They'd compare the quotes and simply take the lowest bid from any shop with a reasonable quality rating. Things were not shaping up as I had planned.

On the home front, Conchita and the kids were acclimating to Florida with mixed success. Conchita shifted her social skills into high gear. She met people at the church and other moms at school. She wasn't happy to be in apartment after leaving our comfortable home in Clifton Springs, but she was patient and supportive. Patricia was feeling much better physically—the asthma was practically gone. Michael was still very young, so I don't remember his having any issues. As for Steven, he was entering first grade. Of course, the schools in Florida were much bigger, as we were not a small village anymore. Not only that, this was his first exposure to a racially diverse classroom. On his first day, the kindly black teacher took Steven's hand to guide him into the classroom, and Steven started yelling his head off! Conchita was mortified. She and the teacher tried to calm him down a little bit, but he was still sobbing. Conchita said he looked at her as if to say, "You're abandoning me here?" It was a shock!

I was so financially clueless that that it wasn't until after I had quit my job and sold my house that I realized that the country was in the middle of a *recession!* In Clifton Springs, we had been sheltered from it. I got my paycheck every month and was doing well professionally, and everything was hunky dory. But the truth was that the recession from 1973 to 1975 in the US and much of the Western world was on such a scale that it occasioned a new phrase: *stagflation* (an unfortunate mingling of high unemployment and high inflation). This called a halt to the economic expansion of the post–World War II era.

When I got to Florida, the machine shop I'd bought started experiencing cancellations of orders because of the effects of the recession. The backlog of business that I had counted on for work while I got the valve design off the ground started shrinking. I was extremely concerned. No orders, no work! After about a year of this fresh hell, I was exhausted—and broke. I was working tirelessly and hardly paying myself a salary. In Clifton Springs, I had been earning about $25,000 a year. Now I was making more like $15,000 or maybe just $12,000 a year.

> *After about a year of this fresh hell,*
> *I was exhausted—and broke.*

Even worse, I hadn't been able to afford a house for Conchita as I'd promised her. Our plan was to take some of the revenue from the Clifton Springs house sale and put a down payment on a home in Florida. But the prices in Florida were double those of rural New York. Even worse, we had to sink all the money into the business. After living in a house for years, we were back in an apartment. Conchita was distraught, and I felt pretty awful myself.

Borrowing money from a bank wasn't an option. I had no house, no savings—only my Rambler station wagon, a money-losing business, and some old machinery. In order to pay my employees, I'd have to get money into the bank so they could cash their checks. There was no "float" per se, and in those days checks took three or four days to cash. Often the workers would have to wait a few days for the money to hit their accounts.

Conchita and I used credit cards to purchase what we needed, but back then the credit card company would cut you off if you didn't pay the balance. Conchita would worry, "Gosh, can we pay this bill?" But she always paid each one, and we always made good. She knew when the shipments were going out and when they were coming in. In forty years we have never had a bounced check.

The service sector made no sense to me as a money-making operation. The biggest problem was maintaining a loyal labor force. If another shop down the road offered my employees a raise of twenty-five cents per hour, they would leave. And big companies like Bendix or United Technologies or Pratt & Whitney were always looking for good people. They'd ask around—"We're looking for a Hardinge operator. You know of any?" And an employee or rep would say, "Oh yes, I think I know someone." And before you knew it, my good Hardinge operator had a job with Pratt & Whitney or Bendix for a little more money. As a designer, I hadn't realized this about the machinists' nickel-and-dime mentality, but now it had become all too clear.

After about a year, I realized that Plan A—letting the machine shop pay the bills while I built my valve business—was tanking. I had to accelerate the valve business. I was digging the hole deeper and deeper. I would go bankrupt if I didn't do something drastic. I decided to call on the companies that I used to work with as an employee at my previous companies, to see if I could interest them in some design work.

I would go bankrupt if I didn't do something drastic.

I had started my business with $50,000, and that was a lot of money to me. Now I don't even think you could start a valve design business with ten times that much. Airline manufacturers don't take risks on new manufacturers. I wasn't new to the industry; with Ronson and Wright Components I had designed valves for some of the biggest companies in the business. Now that I was on my own, these companies would still take my calls—but say no!

I thought my former clients would buy valves from me because I'd worked with them before. But they said, "We can't work with you because you're too small. Management won't accept your design—even though it might be good." The companies knew that before my design was approved, they would have to send out someone to conduct a survey of my company to gauge its ability to make a product for them. I think they would have laughed if they saw my 900-square-foot operation.

All I needed was one contract to get the ball rolling. Cold calls on engineers had always worked well for me in my past jobs. I'd fly or drive to a city where there might be a company that needed valves, then walk into the lobby and say to the nice receptionist, "Can you direct me to a person who buys valves?" And she'll call upstairs and say, "Yes, there is someone. He'll come down and talk to you." Companies were much smaller in those days, and the receptionist would normally have a good idea of who did what. I would show the client some designs, and if he thought there was something he would need, he'd say, "I'll get an engineer to come down and look at it."

On one cold call I went to Woodward Governor in Rockford, Illinois, just outside of Chicago. A manufacturer of control systems and control system components for aircraft engines, Woodward was a company had worked with before, so it was easy to get an appointment. The client said to me, "I know you're a good engineer, but your company is too small. We can't do business with you." I was disappointed, but he suggested, "Why don't you go to Sundstrand Aviation?" That was an aerospace and industrial products company also located in Rockford. The

Woodward engineer even gave me a map of the city so I could find it.

Sundstrand was a huge company, and I had never worked with them before. I just went in, introduced myself, and said, "I'd like to see someone who has valve requirements." And sure enough, someone came down to meet me. Sundstrand designed control systems for other aircraft companies as well as for their own products. They would build entire control systems from components sourced from their plant and others.

The engineer I met with gave me his requirement for a valve he needed. The minute I got back to Florida, I immediately started to design the valve and then sent him a proposal drawing. He said, "Thank you. I'll put it into my report." I didn't know what he meant, but it turned out that Sundstrand was trying to propose a whole system to the client, and my valve was listed as one of the many components in the proposal.

The client was a British company called Dowty Rotol, an aerospace company that specialized in the manufacture, repair, and overhaul of propellers and propeller components for clients around the world. Dowty Rotol was considered a leader in propeller design; they also manufactured aircraft landing gears and other hydraulic components.

Dowty got a contract from British Aerospace to build the flight control system for the BAE 146, a fifty- to ninety-passenger commercial aircraft. But since Dowty wouldn't manufacture all the parts, they contacted the suppliers listed in Sundstrand's proposal to get quotes for the components—so I got a call from Dowty Rotol in England requesting a quote for the valve. I presented Dowty with a price—and they gave me an order for valves to fulfill a dozen of these control systems. Hallelujah—my first aircraft valve contract!

Hallelujah—my first aircraft valve contract!

Our little operation kicked into gear to get those first valves completed, and we shipped them to England. Apparently Dowty was pleased with the result, as the project was put into production.

Often you find yourself depending on people whose kindness is a true gift. I think of Knox Gardner, who went out of his way to assist me in the early days of Valve Research. Another person who helped me grow my business was my old boss and friend Richard Fuller, the general manager at Ronson. We'd kept in touch, and our wives were still friendly. The machinery was outdated at Valve Research, and I needed to purchase a specific tool to fill this important first order—but no bank would help me finance it. I reached out to him, and he said, "I'd be happy to lend you the money." We agreed that I would repay him plus six percent interest when I could. He and his wife were probably more trusting than I was that I would pay it all back in good time—and within a year, I did.

To meet increased production, Dowty had to do a more thorough investigation of each supplier, to make sure they met their quality standards. So their buyer came to Florida from England for a site visit. He walked into my company—remember, it was only a 900-square-foot plant, about the size of my living room now—and he was very surprised!

He looked around and said, "I didn't realize you were so small! If I had known, I wouldn't have given you the order, because we can't afford to take a risk. But," he continued, "because you've produced the product and we bought it, I can't pull it away from you now. Now you're almost qualified for the job!" I believe he never revealed to his bosses the engineer's and buyer's missteps in awarding the initial order for a dozen valves without any survey or audit. It was an honest mistake on their part and a lucky break on mine.

The funny thing is that while Sundstrand's proposal was responsible for that crucial first order, over my career I never got a single order directly from Sundstrand. It was pure luck that their engineer had included my estimate in their proposal for Dowty. When he proposed me, all he knew was that I was a valve supplier. He didn't say or know whether I was a good builder or a bad builder.

The good news was that—as the Dowty buyer had said— since I had proven that I could make the valve they needed for the price they wanted, there was little chance he would go elsewhere. Once you have a client in this field, they tend to be a client for good. It's so costly to qualify suppliers that once a company connects with you as a source for the valve, they tie you down tightly with long-term agreements that dictate price increases and so on for the coming years. This stability allows companies to make projections and, yes, a profit! The aircraft supply business is not competitive in the same way that, for example, the pizza business is. If I don't like a pizza, I'll go somewhere else. In my industry, once a company has the right valve for the right price, the customer doesn't go anywhere else.

> *In my industry, once a company has the right valve*
> *for the right price, the customer doesn't go anywhere else.*

Once I started designing valves again, I started doing less and less of the machine shop work. The shop was making *my* parts, not someone else's. And with my parts, I had better control over the pricing, because I knew exactly how much it would cost.

Now I had a *product* to sell, not just a service to sell. By beginning to produce my valves, I only needed to compete with other valve companies—not small machine shops that usually underbid me and went out of business by doing so! And once

I had a valve design client, I had them for the long haul. Our drawings are proprietary, and neither my customers nor their suppliers could reverse-engineer (copy) my designs without my permission. If they chose to violate the rules, I could sue them. I also had the safety and quality concerns of the aerospace and submersible businesses in my favor. Contracts say that only valves manufactured and rigorously tested by the original manufacturer (often at the cost of $250,000 or more) must be used. All other uncertified valves will be considered counterfeits and unfit for flight.

The Roman philosopher Seneca is quoted as saying, "Luck is what happens when preparation meets opportunity." As I've said, I had done no research into the South Florida region when I bought the business. I had subcontracting work from Dowty Rotol and Bendix, another large manufacturing and engineering company. But now, wanting to keep the lights on, I began to do research about other companies in the area.

I made a cold call on a company called Perry Offshore in Riviera Beach, about thirty miles north of us. The company made oceanographic submersibles, remote-operated vehicles (ROVs) for use underwater. It's a very specific but very profitable business, as ROVs are used by oil companies to service their offshore rigs. At the time, most ROVs were using a lot of industrial valves.

I showed an engineer at Perry Offshore a valve that I'd designed for aircraft, which was much smaller, lighter, and more high-performance than what they were using. They were interested and commissioned a few prototypes. When I delivered them, they fell in love with the product. Conchita even said, "Boy, this is a good industry." They didn't care about the cost because their customers were the oil companies, billion-dollar corporations who wanted very specific valves. I was able to convince them that the aircraft valves were better than the oceanographic valves they were using at the time.

Because of the shortage of oil, the oceanographic industry—which catered to the oil rigs in the Gulf of Mexico, North Sea of Scotland, and around the world—needed submersibles, and they needed them badly. The quantities of valve orders were smaller than I was used to in the aircraft industry, but companies were willing to pay a high price. If they needed something, they'd say, "Pay the supplier whatever he needs so that we can start pumping oil." They were desperate!

Getting involved in the submersible business was a revelation—diversifying my client base.

Getting involved in the submersible business was a revelation—diversifying my client base. I was able to tap into this lucrative market, and it kept us stable when the aircraft industry was going downhill—as it was in the 1970s. When I founded my business, to my dismay I realized that the country was in this terrible recession, and because people were not traveling as much my aircraft valve orders were down. I was still serving clients, but there wasn't as much volume. But the next thing I knew, these ROV manufacturers were buying more valves. The oceanographic business saved me. I knew that I needed both industries, though, because the oil business was extremely volatile. Diversity was the key.

The truth is that I never would have created this revenue stream if I hadn't had the guts to make cold calls. But cold calls had always worked for me when I was working in Charlotte, Dayton, and Clifton Springs. I had the thick skin of a salesman—and the fear that my business would close! I knew that for every ten doors I knocked on, maybe one would turn into a client. I was going to hear a lot of "no" responses, but that didn't matter. I was a gambler, and I liked the odds.

Cold calls had always worked for me. I knew that for every ten doors I knocked on, maybe one would turn into a client.

Sales, especially cold calling, is an art. You have to convince the client that you have a good product. But you must be honest. If I was asked, "Can you build 10,000 valves?" I would say, "No, I can't build that many. But if that number was spread out over ten years, I could." And they would say, "Oh, we don't want all 10,000 in one year. We need 10,000 over the life of the program, which may last at least ten years, if not more." Many of our contracts have lasted decades.

I believe that I was the first designer to introduce aircraft valves into the oceanographic business. Just a few alterations were required, but nothing dramatic. It was a matter of modifying the product to suit the needs. I think my competitors in the aircraft industry probably said, "That's too small an industry. I'm not interested." They would rather stay in their own industry, or possibly the massive automotive industry. But I couldn't build a valve for the automotive industry, because my valve would be too expensive. Of course, I could get to the point where I'd have the capacity to deliver—real estate investments, machine investments, employees—but the automotive industry wasn't of interest to me, and it was already oversaturated with suppliers.

The satellite industry was another field in which the orders were few but prices were high. At Wright Components I had designed solenoid thruster valves for communication satellites to control their antennas, so that they always pointed toward the receiving stations on Earth. But at that time, I was still too small a company. If I wanted to enter that market now, I could, but that would require an additional investment on our part, and I'm careful that we don't spread ourselves too thin.

It was sheer luck that our company was in Florida. It was cheaper to service the oceanographic business because many of the companies were in Florida, just as many of the aircraft companies were in California. And it wasn't a terrible place to hire people; there was a decent labor force of mature workers, including former machinists for Pratt & Whitney, General Electric, and Honeywell.

Transitioning from a machine shop into a manufacturing company making our own products was a difficult period. Much of the original equipment that was bought along with the business was too old and had to be sold. After we upgraded the machinery, our productivity improved and we were able to go into the valve business. At the time these were mostly still manual machines. Numerical controlled (CNC) machines were in their infancy, and we did get some of those as well—but they were just prototypes, so their efficiency was not at all what it is today.

As for workers, I had retained whoever was working there when I purchased the business. The previous owners were two former machinists. One ran a machine and one did sales, but they only stayed for a few months—they weren't comfortable with the changes underway. Some of the employees left for bigger companies; we couldn't compete with higher wages. Every time someone left we had to train another person. Some of them were so-called experienced machinists—but frankly, those experienced machinists couldn't handle these new machines. There was quite a bit of turmoil in those first five years.

Later, when the aircraft industry really started blossoming, we didn't pay as much in time and effort to the oceanographic industry, and it subsided slightly. But I am still involved in both. And I still say to my employees that we should be doing cold calls—though they tell me that that's not necessary!

FLORIDA: THE MIDDLE YEARS, 1979–1990

At the end of our first five years at Valve Research, we got a big order from a submersible ROV company called Ametek-Straza in San Diego, California—a great quantity of manifold valves, resulting in a $120,000 check arriving one day! Conchita and I considered that to be the start of our glory days, because we were able to make a $20,000 down payment on a home on Soleil Circle in Boca Raton. I believe the amount was $95,000. Conchita was the happiest woman in the world! It was a very nice two-story house, with three bedrooms on the ground floor. Patricia had her own room, and the boys bunked together. The living room had cathedral ceilings (my preference), and spiral stairs led to a loft area that I converted into my study.

A Polaroid photo of the manifold for an ROV
(underwater remote operated vehicle) used by the oceanographic
industry, early 1980s. We got an order for 10 of these manifolds,
and used some of the income to make a downpayment on our
first home in Florida. Conchita was thrilled.

At my drafting board in the upstairs loft study in our house on Soleil Circle in Boca Raton, early 1980s.

The rest of the money we poured back into the business. We were outgrowing our 900-square-foot space in Fort Lauderdale. We found an industrial tract of land on Military Trail in Deerfield Beach and built a brand-new 10,000-square-foot building, a tenfold increase in space. It was ambitious—considering that we didn't need most of the space at the time. We filled half of the building with machinery, engineering, and offices. We wanted to rent out the other half but couldn't, because the recession was still ongoing. It took about five years, but our business eventually grew to the point where we were able to use the entire building. We expanded our engineering department and moved assembly onto the other half.

Military Trail location in the 1980s, with some of our early computer programmed (CNC) machines.

The lathe department of the Military Trail location, with computer operated machinery.

We had grown from four machinists to about twenty-five or thirty employees, and we purchased more high-performing machine tools. We had grown not only in the oceanographic field but also in the aircraft field, where we added more customers along with the two that had given us that initial business—Dowty Rotol in England and Hamilton Standard in Connecticut.

Our biggest moneymaker was the solenoid valve—basically an electromagnet in which the magnetic force is used to power the valve. You can just turn a switch on and adjust the power that goes into the valve and it will operate without having to turn a handle. You can command it to do things just by turning on an electrical switch.

I loved having Conchita working at the company, and she was happy to be there. When the kids were in grade school and high school, we would take two cars to work. We'd leave at about the same time, but she would leave work early in the afternoon to be home by the time the kids got back from school.

> *I loved having Conchita working at the company,*
> *and she was happy to be there.*

People would ask if we had any problems working together, but we really didn't! She was in charge of bookkeeping and managing the flow of money, which didn't interest me that much. And I oversaw engineering, which she didn't know anything about. So we never had any conflicts over work. We would check in on the financial situation—in the early days, there were times when we'd have trouble making payroll. We'd pay our company bills and employees and wait on our own bills. That's just how it had to be.

Conchita and me at Patricia's house, 1990s.

*In the offices at Military Trail for a holiday party, 1980s.
From left: a machinist, my son Steven, Conchita,
my secretary Francine Miele, and my son Mike.*

At that time Patricia had left for college at Notre Dame and Michael was at Marquette. Steve was still in high school. This left more time for Conchita to be involved at Valve Research. We didn't have an HR department then, but we did offer such basic benefits as healthcare. We also initiated a bonus system, which has been operating ever since.

As the machinery changed and became computer-based, we tended to seek younger technicians as opposed to the mature machinists that we'd tried so hard to keep. It used to be that we would train a machinist and then big companies would steal them away from us. We'd think, "This person is so important that we can't lose him"—and we then we'd lose him when someone offered him a better job. There was a time when our chief production manager left for another company and we thought, "Now we're in trouble." But we were able to train someone else, and in the end our company didn't suffer.

You should never feel that you are losing someone so important that the company could be in trouble, or that could become true. It's just a matter of perception. People are replaceable. The people we needed ten or twenty years ago aren't the same people we need now! Now we need a younger staff, with their minds wide open, willing to learn new machinery. Again, fortune has worked in my favor. There were schools in South Florida, like Florida Atlantic University and Embry-Riddle, from which we could hire engineers.

You should never feel that you are losing someone so important that the company could be in trouble, or that could become true.

Today we speak in terms of software rather than hardware; we are updating software all the time, and sometimes it requires essentially learning a new language! Being forced to do this kind of regular reprogramming has required me to stay flexible as I've gotten older. The problem with older people, myself included, is that we don't like to change. But sometimes it's good to have a change. It just takes time.

Now, that is not to say that we aren't loyal to employees who have been with us for a long time. We invest in them, and their loyalty yields great returns, even if their skills may be outdated. When they leave, that is the appropriate time to make a change.

I think of Francine Miele, one of our early employees. She was born in Algeria, then moved to France and then French Canada, but she hated the cold. So she moved to Florida. Her husband was a machinist, working for another company. Conchita gave her a job in the office. At first Francine's only job was to type our letterhead on the standard invoice forms we purchased—maybe we were too cheap to get them custom-printed! She typed "*Valve Research and Manufacturing, 466 Military Trail, Deerfield Bch, FL*" on these forms for days. She didn't love the work but said, "That's okay, I don't mind it, because I need the job." Francine had three daughters, was very industrious, and wanted to earn our goodwill. When we first got a computer, she quickly learned how to use it, so that made her work much easier. She was also good at keeping the books. She became a combination secretary, office manager, and production control person, and she became very, very good at what she did. Everyone in the shop liked her because she was so personable. We treated her as if she were our own daughter. She worked at Valve Research for thirty-five years, until she retired. She had been able to amass several hundred thousand dollars in her 401K retirement account—and we gave her a huge bonus as well.

*Conchita and me with my first Jaguar, in Boca Raton
at our Soleil Circle home. Late 80s or early 90s.*

Another person who changed the course of Valve Research was our daughter Patricia. I had always told the kids that I wanted them to work for other companies before I would even consider hiring them at Valve Research. She graduated from Notre Dame with a degree in mechanical engineering and took a job working for a company in Chicago. The company paid for her to study for her MBA part-time at prestigious Northwestern University. She was in a serious relationship with a man named Paul Kilgallon, whom she'd met at Northwestern, and they were thinking about getting married.

I had always told the kids that I wanted them to work
for other companies before I would even consider
hiring them at Valve Research.

About halfway through her MBA studies, Patricia came to me
and said, "Can I come work at the company now?" I said, "Yes,
you may. You have enough background working with someone
else." She decided not to accept her company's offer to continue
paying for her schooling, but she finished her degree and then
moved to Florida to take over the sales manager position at Valve
Research—relieving me of a lot of sales work. Having gotten her
MBA, she had more financial knowledge than I did. And she was
a natural salesperson, very outgoing, and liked to travel. She and
Paul moved in with us until they got married a few months later.
Paul drove Patricia to her first visit to Woodward Governor, and
she won a big valve contract. Afterward we kidded Paul about
being such a great chauffeur!

With Patricia doing sales, I could now focus on the engineering. Conchita did the bookkeeping, and we hired an outside
accountant, Dykes Stevens Accounting Service, which is still the
service we have today.

After Michael graduated from Marquette with a degree in
industrial engineering, he also moved to Chicago and worked
for a year or two. Then he joined Valve Research as vice president of manufacturing. That's when our purchase of state-of-the-
art CNC manufacturing machinery began to expand even more.
Because of his industrial engineering background, we were able
to fill the floors with all the machines that we have now, allowing
us to operate more efficiently.

Growth and expansion depend on a lot more than just
state-of-the-art machinery. First you need machines that have
the appropriate capability do for what you, but then you must
have people who can program them, and then people who can

run them. The first step is actually purchasing the raw materials, which has to be from approved vendors for made-in-the-USA products; that is a requirement for the aircraft industry. Some specialize in stainless steel; others in exotic materials, as we call them; and others in aluminum and low-carbon steels. All material shipped to us must be certified as being made in the USA and must state who the manufacturer was. We are given the chemical analysis of the material as verification. When the material comes in, the parts are fabricated, inspected, and shipped out for subcontract work—like anodizing, heat treating, and plating done by outside vendors. Florida was actually rich in these subcontract support businesses, and we could usually avoid shipping materials out of state to be finished.

Growth and expansion depend on a lot more than just having state-of-the-art machinery.

The parts are then sorted into stores, and when a specific part is needed, it is withdrawn out of storage for assembly by the assembly department. Then the product is inspected again and tested. Of course, inspection is a continuous process from the minute the raw material is received. When a chunk of steel comes in, we even have an instrument that confirms the chemical composition.

Once Mike came on board, I wasn't involved with the quoting anymore. After engineering designs the valve, Mike calculates the estimated time and expense to manufacture it. He presents that proposal to Patricia, the sales manager and now also president, to make sure that it looks like the right price. Then she submits the quote to the customer.

Once we have an established customer, we are the ones they usually come to for first quotes on additional work, and even if our quote is higher than another company's they will choose us because they know we do good work. They'll also refer us to new companies. After ten years or so, we had so many customers regularly sending us new work that we didn't need to make cold calls anymore.

I have learned to embrace new technologies. Buying new software will speed up your job. I can't believe the number of procedures that I used to have to do by hand that are now completed by a machine, or by software. But today I'm more interested in developing ideas or concepts of valves rather than building them. I let the production manager figure that part out!

I have learned to embrace new technologies.

Speaking of embracing new technologies, when I was about fifty years old I decided to try something that I had dreamed about since I was a child: learning to fly. Conchita was supportive and encouraged me to give it a try. I signed up for lessons at a flight school located at the Boca Raton Airport, not far from our home. I learned how to control an airplane—how to take off, maintain speed, maintain altitude, and use some of the instruments. After taking a few courses, I flew in a Cessna 152 with a trainer as the copilot; she taught me how to land and take off. The exercise is called "touch and go"—you land and touch ground briefly and then take off again. (The Cessna 152 has fixed landing gear, which makes it easier for practice.) I learned to fly around the airport and how to overcome a stall. I actually found flying was quite easy, and I enjoyed it.

But the better I got, the more I understood that there's a lot more to being a pilot than just flying an airplane. You have to know the regulations as you approach and depart the airport.

You have to communicate with the tower, which I found difficult both due to the noise of the engine and also the flight lingo. It was also expensive, about $50 plus the cost of gas every time I went up. At the end of the training, you have to "fly blind," using only your flight instruments, and that scared me. I was also concerned about my family and my business, should there be an accident. I thought, "Why don't I return to this when I am retired?" But of course, when you retire, you're almost too old to fly! However, I had learned how to land and take off and understood how to control the airplane. My lust for flying was satisfied.

Over the years we hired several salesmen in different parts of the world—but frankly, most of the European salespeople weren't productive for us. I found American salespeople to be much more industrious; they're more outgoing and goal-oriented. And because of the globalization of industries in recent years, many of our customers are doing both engineering and manufacturing abroad and are buying our valves directly, without our having to hire salespeople to promote them.

So as Valve Research grew, we did become a global company, not of our own accord but because of customers with global subsidiaries outside of the USA. And we began to manufacture products not just for US companies but for international clients as well. Today we are building products with both commercial and military aircraft clients. We also ship valves to our customers' subcontractors in other parts of the world—including the Philippines, of all places! One client, the motion control company Moog, has a plant there. We also have our products finished by other companies, not all of whom are located in the US. We ship products to the UK, Switzerland, Germany, New Zealand, India, Israel, the Philippines, and Vietnam to fulfill orders for American companies assembling products in those countries. Shipping costs are not an issue; most of our valves are lightweight and can be shipped in considerable quantities via air freight.

When I think about how our business has changed, I think of the increase in paperwork required before a company can award a contract. We must build the cost of satisfying these requests into the valve price. There are all kinds of surveys that each company conducts to make sure we meet their specific requirements. But we also must adhere to standards set by the International Organization for Standardization (ISO). This non-governmental third-party organization publishes quality standards for aircraft manufacturing, and these have been widely adopted by suppliers serving the aerospace industries worldwide. All our products must meet these standards, a process that is time-consuming and expensive. This is a necessary requirement, however, and it keeps us in good standing with our clients, many of whom we've dealt with for decades. Many companies have changed names, many have changed ownership, and some of the older companies have sold off certain divisions. United Technologies was once Hamilton Standard; now it's Raytheon Technologies.

When I think about how our business has changed,
I think of the increase in paperwork required
before a company can award a contract.

But here's the good news—when companies splintered into other companies, we'd get several new clients out of one! We might not have to make cold calls anymore, but I still like to go and visit new customers and show them new products. When you visit people, they give *you* ideas on *your* business. You think, "Maybe I could adopt some of those processes." Or they'll say, "Why don't you do it this way?" You learn from that conversation and the back-and-forth, but it's not that common anymore.

During the COVID pandemic, the fact that Valve Research had diversified into several industries kept us afloat. Of course, the commercial aircraft industry came to a standstill, as flights were grounded for months. But thanks to our work with military programs, we were considered an essential business and could keep our doors open. We also used the time to build up a larger inventory of goods in our finished parts store, so that we'd be ready to go when the commercial aircraft industry ramped back up (and it has). The year 2021 was our lowest year in recent history due to the pandemic, but it didn't hurt us personally or professionally. We were able to keep all our employees on salary, though overtime was reduced.

Over the years, military contracts—like oceanographic submersibles—have been a small but lucrative revenue stream for us. The valves we design are the same whether they are used for commercial or military aircraft. One of our longtime clients is General Dynamics' combat systems division. Our valves are used for armored tracked vehicles used in land support. About ten years ago we got a US military contract for a particular valve. Then the Israeli government asked us to build a valve for a specific gun control. Then the Israelis and the US got together and said, "Okay, we're going to build the same gun." So now this valve is being bought by both countries.

The military orders are small but longstanding. Once the government develops a certain gun, they'll build 200 of them one year and put them in storage. And then with the next year's budget they'll build more of the same guns and put them in storage—or, unfortunately, use them. Sometimes you hate to think what a military order implies. For example, recently we had a reorder for valves placed on missile-launching vehicles that the US is probably providing to Ukraine in the Russo-Ukranian War. And they're probably killing a lot of young Russians who don't even know why they are at war; the Russian government is not truthful in its war efforts. Military defense is a necessary evil, but I'm glad that our valves are contributing to the strength of the US and its allies.

Many of our contracts last for decades. I'm still building airplane valves for the Boeing 707, a contract I got a year or two after I founded Valve Research. The orders aren't for great quantities, but if the original price for the valve was $400, it's now $4,000. These days it's considered a custom order, and we have to make a special run to fill the order.

The aircraft industry is protected from these exponential price increases because the materials are still considered a small expense in their business. The larger costs in the airline industry are for the aircraft, labor, and fuel. To replace a spare part that costs $3,000 versus a onetime cost of $300 is peanuts; it's an infrequent occurrence and is passed along to the consumer. But the commercial aviation industry must remain competitive, and new planes cannot become too expensive. The military is another story—it seems that all they do is go to the "government printing office" and print out more money!

FLORIDA: 1990s

As Valve Research hit its ten-year and fifteen-year anniversaries, it continued to expand. When I turned fifty-five in 1990, I began to feel that Conchita and I should start enjoying some of the fruits of our labors. We had begun to attend the Farnborough Air Show in London and the Paris Air Show, the largest international shows devoted to aircraft and space, held biannually on alternating years. Our ROV business also took us to Aberdeen in Scotland, the oil industry's center of operations for the North Sea. I reflected on how far Conchita and I had come since our college dates to the Manila airport to watch the planes take off and land!

With all the kids having graduated from college and the business maintaining a steady rise, Conchita and I thought about a trip to Egypt. As important as money was to me—keeping the business going, paying for my home and my children's educations—I was not motivated by it. Saving for the future was crucial, but money was also something to be spent and enjoyed.

Saving for the future was crucial, but money was also something to be spent and enjoyed.

I had stayed good friends with Ray Ganowsky, my former colleague from Clifton Springs when I worked for Wright Components. A mechanical engineer like myself, he and his wife Melzie had moved to St. George, Utah, at about the same time that we moved to Boca Raton. He had also started a solenoid and later a valve company, called Ram Companies, but we hardly ever competed since he concentrated on the West Coast and I concentrated on the East Coast. (That isn't the case anymore.) If we happened to share a client, we agreed that since we were competitors, we shouldn't discuss any work issues relating to that client. Still, it was nice to have someone with whom to discuss personal and professional issues.

Conchita and me with Ray and Melzie Ganowsky. We traveled with them often. Could be Lake Powell or Lake Mead.

Back in the '80s, when Patricia was in her sophomore year of college, we ran into a problem paying for her tuition. Even though she was at Notre Dame, it wasn't a lot of money, but it was still a problem. Since Valve Research wasn't yet paying me enough of a salary to cover her tuition, we had to borrow money through a second mortgage of our home. I think that was the only time that Conchita asked me, "Was starting this business really the right decision?"

I kept saying, "Yes, just hold on. The ship is not sinking yet." The truth was that the ship was listing a little bit. But we just had to patch up the holes and keep going. When I told Ray of my troubles, he'd said that he'd mortgaged his home several times. He was in worse trouble than I was!

But this was about ten years later, and both my company and Ray's were on solid ground. When Conchita and I decided to go on an overseas trip, we asked Ray and Melzie to join us. And we would say for the rest of our lives that our first trip to Egypt was the best trip we'd ever taken. People would ask, "What's so special about Egypt?" All I could say was, "You have to go there to appreciate it." But I also think I was in desperate need of a vacation!

We stayed in an elegant historic hotel in Cairo called the Mena House. Originally a royal lodge, it was purchased by a wealthy British couple and turned into a glamorous hotel in 1886. Its forty acres of gardens lay in the shadows of the Pyramids of Giza. We used the hotel as our luxurious base of operations while we traveled around Egypt for two weeks. It was spectacular.

The success of that trip led to our golden years of travel. In addition to London and Paris for the air shows, Conchita and I traveled through Norway and Sweden. We traveled to Alaska, including a cruise to witness glacier-calving—which is when chunks of ice break of at the end of a glacier, creating icebergs. Conchita's family all still lived in the Philippines, so she would visit them every few years. Her "rich sister" Tessie and her husband Tony would visit us whenever they had a chance.

I also introduced Conchita to another hobby of mine—gambling! In Florida we had casinos not far from our home, and I always enjoyed playing blackjack. At first Conchita would just play the slot machines, as most people do. But then she real-ized that the slot machines were just taking her money. "I put in $20, and it lasted me one hour," she'd say. "I had fun, but I never win." Occasionally she might get the jackpot and win $400, which was fine, but that was once in a blue moon.

At the table games, you could make some money if you knew how to play. So she started learning how to play blackjack. I'd usually budget $2,000 a visit for myself, but she would say, "Just give me $200." Instead of playing $25 a chip, she'd play the $10 tables. Before long she'd learned how to play and hold on to her winnings, or reduce her losses to a minimum. Conchita enjoyed it, and our money—my $2,000, her $200—would last equally as long. We were both happy! Of course, Las Vegas was our favorite destination. We'd go at least twice a year, and we'd also visit Ray and Melzie in St. George, about two hours away. Or they would meet us in Vegas. But they didn't enjoy gambling, so they would spend their time in Vegas shopping or going to shows. Conchita and I would meet them to go see some of the shows, but we spent most of our evenings at the casinos.

We also went to Macau, which I considered my ancestral country but now is known for its high-stakes gambling. However, our arrival fell right on the Chinese New Year, so we had trouble getting a hotel! Luckily I had a high-roller account at the Wynn in Vegas. When I called them to ask for help finding with a hotel room in Macau, the Wynn there was full but they put us up at the gorgeous Mandarin Oriental.

Conchita and I were well matched. We were different people, but we enjoyed each other's company and got to know each other's likes and dislikes. We continued to spend time with two couples who'd been among our best friends since moving to Florida. Interestingly, we'd met these couples the same way we'd met our best friends in Charlotte and Dayton—by living in the same apartment building. When we moved to Florida, we first lived in Boca Center Apartments off Palmetto Park Road, and that's where we met Dan and Jan Gewartowski and Fred and Odesa Bauman. Dan became our family dentist. Fred worked for Prudential Securities and eventually became my stockbroker—once I had money to invest! The six of us would have dinner or play cards together at least once a month.

Conchita and I were very well matched;
we enjoyed each other's company and got to know
each other's likes and dislikes.

Conchita joined up with the mothers' bowling group at Pope John Paul II High School when Steven was a student there, and we met a lot of their children and husbands through that connection. She was also active at St. Jude Church, and I volunteered for the St. Jude Hunger Program. The group would collect donations for hunger programs both domestically and internationally. When I served as chairman, I suggested Our Lady of Sorrows Parish, my former church in Manila, as an outreach candidate. Ever since then, St. Jude has sent them a couple thousand dollars a few times a year—and that goes a long way in the Philippines.

While my father had died too young, in his early sixties, my mother lived to be ninety-three. Living in Toronto with my sister Olivia, she worked as an electronic assembler at Motorola. We would visit her occasionally, or she would come down to Florida. For her eighty-fifth birthday we all traveled to Toronto and had a big party to celebrate. I still have the family photo.

*With my siblings Joe, John, and Olivia at our mother's
85th birthday in Toronto.*

She and my father were happy in Canada. It had been an adventure for them to move there from the Philippines. They liked being relatively near their children, and they were able to find steady work. In the last few years of my mother's life, my sister was still working as a teacher, but my mother's health had deteriorated to a point where she couldn't be home alone. So my siblings and I said, "Mother, you have to go to a nursing home and be taken care of." Of course, she objected vehemently. But she finally agreed, realizing it was unsafe to be by herself at home. About five years later, in 2001, she died at the nursing home. We buried her next to my father at Mount Hope cemetery in Toronto.

At the end, my mother had struggled with dementia. For decades, when I came to visit she would say, "How's your business doing?" Whether we were doing well or not, I would say, "We're having some rough times here and there, but everything is great." I didn't want to stress her out. When I moved to Florida, my mother and others would ask, "Have you met any millionaires yet?" I would say, "No, I haven't rubbed elbows with one yet. I don't think there are that many here." She would tease, "But there are lots of rich people in Florida." I replied, "Well, unfortunately I'm still maybe too poor to rub elbows with a millionaire."

Toward the end of her "good days," my mother asked me how I was doing. I was able to say, "I'm doing very well. I think I'm going to make a million dollars very soon." Being a millionaire was to her the ultimate. "But a million dollars is not actually what I have in the bank or in my hands," I explained. "I have a million dollars in terms of assets." And she asked, "What are assets?" "Well," I said, " like machinery in the company, and the building itself." And she said, "Oh, I understand." She was very proud and pleased.

When my mother died, I was glad she had known that my business was a success. She was a very smart woman. She had always pushed her children to do well in school and to get a college education, as she and my father had not been fortunate enough to do. I will always be grateful to her for that.

> *When my mother died, I was glad she had known*
> *that my business was a success.*

Being an old-fashioned person, my mother wanted to be able to leave something to her children when she died. She had earned some equity in Motorola, and the Canadian social security system is generous, so she had been able to save some money. When she passed away, her savings were distributed equally among the four kids. Her house was transferred to Olivia's name, but everything else we divided up. I gave the cash I received to Conchita and said, "Buy yourself something nice in memory of my mother." She purchased a lovely ruby pendant.

FLORIDA: THE LATER YEARS, 2000–TODAY

Around the year 2000, not only Conchita, Patricia, Mike, and I were employed at Valve Research, but Steven came on board as well. Unlike my older two children, Steven was not an engineer. He had graduated from the University of Miami and founded his own graphic design business. But as I have argued previously, this business is service-driven, not product-driven, and the competition for clients is fierce. When Steve finally asked if he could join the company, since he was not an engineer I told him, "The only job I have for you is in human resources." It wasn't a great-paying job, but he understood that. It's not an easy job, either! But now, twenty years later, I am happy that he is on board.

*Conchita and me in the lobby at the
40th anniversary party, 2014.*

With all of the grandchildren at the 40th anniversary party:
Emily, Julie, Paul, Hannah, Lindsay, and Jack.

Conchita and Patricia in 2014, at our 40th anniversary party.

As we get older, we want to hold on to our goodies. But then we realize that we're growing older and that eventually everything we have is going to go to the kids anyway. So why not give it to them while you are still alive? There are the economics of estate planning to consider as well. Before Valve Research reached a certain valuation, at which the kids would suffer from inheritance tax, Conchita and I said, "Why don't we just transfer our stock ownership to them, so they don't have to worry about having to pay exorbitant taxes when we pass on?"

We began the process of the stock transfer, but there was a major issue. One share of Valve Research stock was owned not by me but by—Knox Gardner! When Knox had helped me buy the business thirty years before, I'd given him that one share in lieu of payment, which he had accepted—reluctantly—and stashed the note away in a folder. The attorney structuring the stock transfer said to me, "You have to try to buy the share back from him."

Knox and I had not kept up in recent years. He and Norma had divorced decades ago and Conchita and I had tried to remain friends with both of them, but it had been difficult. I had basically lost touch with him, and it took me a while to find him. We discovered that he was living in Fort Knox, Kentucky, and was remarried. I finally located a phone number and gave him a call. I told Knox that we were transferring full ownership to the kids, and I said, "You remember that share?" He said, "Yes, I do. But I don't think I can find it anymore because Norma took everything." Not only that, but Norma had passed away. Knox said, "For me to go and try to get that stock certificate is almost impossible. Either Norma burned it, or she gave it to her daughters. They will not want to give it to me. I don't know what to do."

I told him I'd talk it over with my attorney, who responded that the solution was easy. All he had to do was send Knox a letter to sign, whereby he would forfeit any further claim. At that time, we still hadn't figured out how much Knox's one share was worth. We had hired an independent company to value ours, and its evaluation was still being conducted. We were surprised when the company reported a value of $120,000 per share! I said to the children, "I'm going to transfer my stock to you. You don't have to pay me anything. The only thing you have to do is pay Knox back." So they each paid him about $40,000.

One day Knox's wife opened a letter. She said to him, "It's for a check for $120,000, from someone named Paul Cruz!" Knox was flabbergasted. He called me and said, "I can't accept this." And I said, "No, you earned it!"

I could have just told the lawyer, "Sorry, I can't find this guy." Knox and I had indeed lost touch. But he had been integral to the launching of my business. He had evaluated properties and traveled with me to Florida. He even came back down to Florida a few years after I had launched the business to check up on me—all of it at his own expense.

The irony was, as he was an accountant like my father, Knox hadn't made much money in his own career. Just as my father had cautioned, he was counting someone else's money. And he was retired at that time. But Knox was able to buy himself a new SUV with the windfall from the Valve Research stock purchase, and he drove all the way down to Florida to thank me. He and his second wife then drove to Key West. He told me, "I've been wanting to go to Key West all my life. And now with this money, I'm able to go." Unfortunately, Knox was a heavy smoker, and within two or three years he passed away. But at least I felt that our friendship and this repayment had allowed him to enjoy his later years a bit more.

How did Conchita's and my life change when we became wealthy? As we had both come from relatively poor backgrounds, I don't think it is possible that money would ever have been completely off our minds. And I very much enjoyed working, so I had no intention of retiring. Conchita continued to come into the office a few days a week as well. But whenever we had the opportunity to travel, we took it.

As we got a little older, however, Conchita began to have some concerns about traveling. It was not so much a fear of a plane crash or a car accident—though those thoughts did bother her. But she became overly concerned with travel difficulties: missed flights, lost luggage, vanished hotel reservations. When we were younger, she'd have said, "Well, we'll just keep driving until we see a Holiday Inn or a Howard Johnson's." We would drive and drive until we got tired, and then we'd stop. Sure enough, there was always a room. Now that we could afford to stay at the Four Seasons or Ritz Carlton, the Wynn in Las Vegas, the Peninsula in Hong Kong, and the Royal York in Toronto, and to visit places we'd always dreamed about, Conchita had become less interested in traveling.

I was little disappointed that Conchita had lost the travel bug. But we began to see a lot of our friends buy second homes—cottages in North Carolina or Georgia, for example—and considered that as an option. Friends would say, "You should get a place here. You've got the money." I certainly thought about it. But these vacation homes were a long way from South Florida; they'd visit them only two or three times a year. I needed to be closer to my business; I couldn't be away for long. It just wasn't a practical option.

So then Conchita and I thought, why not just buy something nearby? We both liked the beach. Ever since we'd moved to Florida, I'd gotten into the habit of driving over to the beach a few mornings a week to take a walk. Or sometimes I'd go in the evenings after work. I'd walk for about forty-five minutes, sometimes longer. Our five-bedroom, four-and-a-half-bath house with a swimming pool, on Via Marbella in West Boca Raton, was about five miles from the ocean. I would drive to the pavilion at the public beach at Palmetto Park Road and A1A, then park and walk barefoot in the ocean for miles. Conchita would occasionally join me.

I liked to walk on the beach for a few reasons. One was for the exercise. And one was unexpected. I had suffered my entire life from athlete's foot, and no cure had ever worked. But once I started walking the beaches, it went away. Maybe it was the saltwater that cured it—I can't be sure. But since then, I've never had any problem.

Another reason I liked to walk was that it relaxed me. It allowed me to unburden my mind and to see things in a different way. When I walk, my mind is still working on my designs. I'd say that walking has helped me work through problems and roadblocks many times! Even at age 88, I still walk on the beach a few times a week.

Walking on the beach relaxed me; it allowed me to unburden my mind and to see things in a different way.

About ten years ago, my daughter Patricia bought a one-bedroom condo across the street from the ocean in Delray Beach, which she and her husband, Paul, used as a weekend place. They invited us to use it one weekend, and Conchita and I loved it. We enjoyed seeing the ocean from the apartment windows and thought, "We should really think about getting a place like this." I had walked these beaches many times, but I'd never paid much attention to the many condo buildings lining the shore. Paul told me, "There is a really nice condo available on A1A, right near Palmetto Park Road, where you used to walk." "Really?" I asked.

It was an apartment in Ocean Reef Towers, a modern white-washed building right on the water. So I made an appointment to see it.

When you walked in the front door, all you could see was the ocean. The penthouse condo had floor-to-ceiling windows that wrapped around the perimeter. It felt as if we were on a cruise ship, way up high, looking down at the water. It was as if the room were a ship's bow, breaking through the waves. It reminded me of my ocean adventures on freighters and cruise ships, and all the excitement and promise of those journeys; and all the good times we had spent traveling. I loved it.

As we were walking out the door, the sales agent said, "Well, do you like it?" I said, "Yes, I do. I'm going to make you an offer right now." Conchita was surprised! Prior to that we'd seen at least a dozen places, and they'd all been about the same price. I was getting tired of looking,

I'll admit that I am a bit of an impulse buyer. Whether it's a pair of shoes or even a condo, when I see what I want, I get it. I hate to shop! Some people would say, "If you want this pair of shoes, go to five different stores and you'll get them at the best price." I never cared to do that. I said to Conchita, "Let's make the owner an offer." So we went to talk privately, and I said, "Let's just offer $1 million." The agent called the owner and then said, "They want a bit more." I said, "All right: $1.1 million with the furniture." The next day the offer was accepted—that's how quick it was!

Later, when I met some of my new neighbors, they were astonished that the condo had sold for more than $1 million; other condos in the building had gone for close to that price, but not over. They said, "You are the one who broke the million-dollar mark." And I said, "I didn't know. I thought I was being fair." "Oh no," one said. "You could have gotten it for less." "Well, too late," I said. But what happened then? Everyone started selling their condos for more than $1 million! They said, "Thanks to Paul Cruz, we can make a little more money!" And even though I could now sell the condo for much more than I bought it for, I'm not interested in leaving.

Conchita and I enjoyed the new apartment very much. When we were younger, whenever we had friends visit from the Philippines, New York, or elsewhere, we had always taken them for a drive up and down the coastline. And, of course, we would always say, "It would be nice to live here." But at the time we weren't even close to being able to afford it.

When we bought the penthouse, I said to Conchita, "Isn't that funny? We said to people that this is where we wanted to be. And now here we are." It was one of those moments—when you finally achieve something you've been talking and dreaming about your whole life. We used to look up at these oceanfront buildings and wonder who lived there, and now *we* were living in one of them. We felt very thankful that we had gotten the opportunity.

> *It was one of those moments—when you finally achieve something you've been talking and dreaming about your whole life.*

After work on Friday, our new routine was to load up the car with groceries, leave our home in West Boca, and drive over to the condo for the weekend. It was so close geographically, but it was a completely different environment, a new life entirely. Maybe most people wouldn't understand having a second home so close to their first—taxes on two homes, furniture, utilities, expenses. But Conchita and I agreed that the condo was a good idea. "We have the money," she said, "so let's go and spend it." Conchita was very, very good about that. Even though I would sometimes buy things without looking at the price tag, she was so confident about our financial situation that she didn't let it bother her. I was glad she felt that security and comfort.

A recent photo of the "new building" in Newport Center Industrial Park.

Conchita passed away on September 26, 2018, at the age of eighty-four. It happened so quickly: she had a series of strokes, and a month later she was gone. I like to think that because it happened so fast, she didn't suffer much. Sometimes I wonder if I could have done something differently to extend her life. But I never realized that the end could come so soon. I had been in hospitals before, with my mother, for example, but I was not prepared when Conchita died.

Conchita had had high cholesterol and had been prescribed medication for that, but it was difficult for her to take because it made her sick. Eventually she convinced the doctor that the medication was not an option, but she was careful about her diet. I often wonder if her tendency toward perfectionism caused stress in her body; she always wanted everything done correctly and would get upset if it wasn't. She was like my mother in that way, while I was more like my dad—more laid back.

One night, Conchita and I went to a Mexican restaurant with the Gewartowskis and the Baumans. The two of us were seated side by side at a high-top table. After dinner, Conchita started sliding onto my chair. I propped her up as she said, "I don't know what's going on. I feel like I'm losing control of my body." "Maybe you're just tired," I said. "Yes," she responded, "That must be it." We continued our conversation, but as we walked to our car she said, "Stay close to me in case I lose my balance." I thought she might be coming down with some virus.

The next morning, Conchita had that funny feeling again, as if something was wrong. I immediately called the doctor and made an appointment for later that morning. Conchita said, "Well, let's go to work until then." Though we normally drove our own cars, I drove her to her office at its Military Trail location and then went to mine at Newport Center.

Almost immediately Steven called and told me, "Mother's talking funny." I called the doctor, and he said to go to the emergency room right away. After some tests, they discovered that Conchita had had a minor stroke. She was admitted to the hospital and stayed there for three days. It seemed too soon for her to go home, but they prescribed physical therapy for her lost control and movement and arranged for our home to be checked for any necessary accommodations.

After only two days at home, Conchita had another episode. We went immediately to the hospital, and they discovered that she that she had had a second stroke, with much more devastating effects. Before long she couldn't even stand, had no appetite, and eventually lost kidney function. She had to be transferred to Bethesda Hospital in Delray Beach for extensive therapy. She would not have wanted kidney dialysis, but by that point she was only semiconscious. After one day on a dialysis machine, she passed away.

In the hospital, Conchita had said to one of our friends, "I know I'm dying. But I think I had a very good life." I wish she would have said that to me, but she deteriorated so quickly that she was almost comatose within weeks. Of course, there is more I wish we could have said to each other, but it's true that she and I had had a very good life. Until the end, Conchita lived life to the fullest. Even though she didn't need to, she continued to come to the office a few days a week. For thirty years she bowled every Thursday with her "Lady Popers." She doted on her nine grandchildren, taking them on shopping sprees to the Boca Town Center mall. She attended mass at St. Jude's every Sunday.

Until the end, Conchita lived life to the fullest.

Conchita's passing came as a complete shock to me, as well as our children and friends. The time from her first stroke to her passing was only about one month. All along I had been thinking, "People get strokes all the time. They recover. Why shouldn't she?" But she was such a small, birdlike woman, with very little body fat, and once she began to falter, she had no reserve to draw on.

I wished that Conchita would have recovered and, with therapy, have gotten back to normal. But I couldn't help thinking that she would have never liked to be imprisoned in a dialysis machine. It was so confusing that up until her first stroke she had been so energetic and vibrant, even that last day at work.

I try not to dwell on Conchita's passing, because there's nothing that can be done. But I miss her. At the time it did trouble me that in the turmoil of her final days, I'd completely forgotten to call the priest and have him administer the Last Rites to Conchita in the hospital. As Conchita and I were raised Catholic, administering the sacraments of Confession, Anointing of the Sick, and Communion to a dying person was understood to be a must. When it dawned on me that I had forgotten, I was very upset.

I called Father John from St Jude's and told him of my concern. "Don't worry," he said. "Conchita was such a good woman. St. Peter will let her right through the gates of Heaven." He told me that saying prayers for her in the funeral mass would suffice. I appreciated his words.

The funeral at St. Jude was packed. Next to me were Patricia and Paul; Michael and his wife, Karen; Steven and his wife, Diana; and our grandchildren—Michelle, Brian, Emily, Julie, Hannah, Jack, Lindsay, Paul, and Kyle—as well as other family members. There were rows and rows of friends, business associates, acquaintances from church or from the kids' schools—dozens and dozens of people, each of whom considered Conchita one of their closest friends. We held a beautiful reception afterward at Delray Dunes Country Club.

Conchita and me in 2017 at the
Delray Dunes Country Club.

I went back to our home on Via Marbella. But after a few weeks I decided that the large house was too much of a burden to take care of, especially now that I had the condo to maintain as well. Conchita had been so good at taking care of our home. She knew exactly where every bill was, whom to pay and when. I was getting frustrated because I had to pay several late penalties on my bills. I didn't want to deal with it. So I thought, why don't I put the house up for sale and then take all the treasures and put them in the condo, or give them to the kids? The rest of it we could put in storage or give away. And that's what I did.

Conchita was proud of the business we had built together, but above all she was proud of our children. Conchita was a college graduate and a businesswoman, but she was a wife and mother first. She was proud of Patricia, who has become a very good businessperson, very strict about toeing the line—much stricter than I am! If Patricia tells me that something must be done, I say, "Okay, you're steering this ship now. So you decide." I have designated that she is the "Iron Lady" of the company.

Conchita was proud of the business we had built together, but above all she was proud of our children.

Mike is an outgoing person, much like Conchita. Steven is also like Conchita, more willing to bend a little with fellow employees. My kids have worked hard, but they never felt the financial strains that Conchita and I went through. Though they witnessed our struggles, they didn't experience them personally—just as I witnessed my parents struggle in life. I could see my father having problems keeping a job, and it taught me a lot. I never had that problem in my own career. I always left the company if my departure were imminent, rather than being laid off.

I was never much for hobbies. I never took up golf—it was too frustrating and too time consuming. I like to travel, and still do. Within the past two years I've gone to Germany, Italy, Canada, California. I'm fascinated by history and keep informed on politics. I like to gamble a few nights a month, and I still walk and work out with a trainer. I have dinner with the Gewartowskis and Baumans and other friends, and I see my family often.

At the age of 88, I still go to the office five days a week, and I still enjoy it! Work is a blessing. I love that I have something important to do. Otherwise, how would I spend my time—sit and watch television all day? I'm fortunate that I can work with my family, and I have longtime clients that I know and projects to design. Aside from the monetary reward, there is the intellectual reward of my work.

Work is a blessing. I love that I have something important to do. Otherwise, how would I spend my time?

That said, I didn't hold my intellectual property close to the vest by filing for patents. I found the process more of a nuisance than it was worth. At Valve Research we have never put a design up for a patent. The elements that I use, such as valve seats or balls used to shut off valves, have been around for decades. The design reliability depends on simplicity—you have to create simple designs. If you design a monstrosity, it might do the same job but it's not as reliable. The more parts you have in any design, the more the reliability of the design goes down and the expense goes up.

If I did take the time and expense to have my designs patented, I would have to challenge anyone who copied them.

That's where additional costs come in, and sleepless nights thinking about it. I thought, "I'm not going to subject myself to that legal nonsense just to protect my patents." So I decided not to patent my designs, and no one has ever sued me for stealing *their* patents. Nothing that I've used is patentable anymore. What I do that *is* valuable is designing a valve that uses all of its elements in the most efficient and most reliable way.

2017: PAUL L. CRUZ
SCHOLARSHIP PROGRAM

In Conchita's and my later years, with our children grown, our business on solid footing, and finding ourselves wealthier than I could ever have imagined, I began to think about giving back and providing for the next generation. I've concluded that I'm not a person who likes to make money just for the sake of it. I consider money as a tool, a vehicle for doing good. As a young man, husband, and father, of course I wanted to ensure that my family was well fed and cared for. But my family is now well off, and I have given my children the business. My intention is to leave a portion of my stocks and real estate investments to charity and to divide the rest equally between the three children, just as we did with the company. How much, I don't know—I'm not dead and buried yet! Not only that, I am trying to set an example for my children for using their money as a tool not just for themselves, but for others.

I'm not a person who just likes to make money for the sake of it. I consider money as a tool, as a vehicle to do good.

In 2017, Conchita and I took a trip to the Philippines to visit her sisters. I visited De La Salle University, my alma mater, and was impressed with how the school had expanded and grown. The university is renowned for its academic excellence, productive and relevant research departments, and community service, and it is now attended by both local and international students seeking a quality education for a brighter future. It now has eight schools on its campus, thirty-six academic departments, eleven research departments, and about 11,000 students. The campus—with its green lawns, modern buildings and large sports complex—now stretches for blocks.

I thought back to the time when I was a student at De La Salle and had to go to the dean's office and tell him that my father didn't have the money to pay the tuition for my brother and me. The dean had generously allowed us to enroll anyway. But in all the decades since, I had never learned whether my father had ever paid them back. None of our friends at the time knew that we were attending without paying. It had been a source of shame for my family and me. And I had never wanted to ask my father about it in case he was still feeling ashamed. Even after he died, I never asked my mother either. I thought, why do I want to bring up these bad things that happened to us in the past? I never even asked my brother John if he knew what had happened.

I certainly didn't blame my father for his inability to pay our tuition years ago. We didn't have a luxurious childhood. It was always struggle, struggle, struggle. And even though my father always found employment, he was never paid well. He was not a college or even a high school graduate; he had had to leave high school at the age of fourteen. He learned how to be an accountant just by the force of his own will.

Even though our unpaid tuition wasn't my father's fault, I still sensed that my family found it shameful. But when I began to share about that part of my history to my friends here in America, they said, "Your story is no different than what my father went through in this country." One friend said, "My father struggled, too. He had to drive a cab because his job didn't pay him enough to make ends meet. We children didn't feel ashamed—we thought it was perfectly normal. Everyone struggled." Another friend grew up in the American South in a house with no flush toilets, just an outhouse. Many others were raised during the Great Depression with very little to eat. Again, I was surprised, as I still thought of the streets of America as being paved in gold. But in truth, America is a country of immigrants, and struggle for immigrants, sadly, is commonplace. But it is also true that it is still a mecca of unlimited opportunities for those willing to expand their capabilities.

Since I would never be able to learn whether my father had paid our tuition, I decided that I would repay it on my own, in my own way. Inspired by my visit to the modern-day De La Salle University—and grateful for the education I received there—I endowed the school with the Paul L. Cruz Scholarship Grant in 2017, providing four full scholarships for mechanical engineering students from first year to graduation. Eligibility requirements include a GPA of at least 3.0; no grades lower than 2.0; a good moral character; and demonstrated need (evidenced through a bio, financial information, and a photo of their family residence). Scholars are required to maintain at least a 2.5 GPA.

As I departed his office, the president of De La Salle University inquired what had prompted me to donate and set up a scholarship program. I told him about what the Christian Brothers had done for me when my father lost his job. He chuckled and said, "They most probably are celebrating up there today."

I'm not ashamed anymore to reveal that my parents struggled. Hopefully it gives some readers—or one of my scholarship students or maybe a young entrepreneur—an idea of what my family had to go through for me to end up where I am today. Hopefully some of my scholars might one day reflect on their own difficult past and be inspired to emulate what I've accomplished. And while our charitable trust is self-sustaining, I hope that my children and grandchildren will become interested in growing it even more.

I'm not ashamed anymore to reveal that my parents struggled. Hopefully it gives some readers—or one of my scholarship students or maybe a young entrepreneur— an idea of what my family had to go through for me to end up where I am today.

Conchita and I always found it important to give back to our employees at Valve Research as well. I think one of the reasons we had very low turnover throughout the years is not only that we paid good salaries but also that we instituted our own version of a bonus system. Most companies pass out bonuses once a year, and for two or three years we did the same, giving each employee a bonus at Christmastime. But we found that while the employees were excited to get their bonuses, by the next month it was all gone; they would have bought a new car or gone on vacation. For the rest of the year, the employees would be just humming along and maybe not pushing as hard as they should. So we thought about trying something different.

We gathered the staff and said, "If we make a good profit this quarter, we're going to give you a good bonus." We called it the bonus pool. Forty years later the bonus pool is now somewhere around $50,000 a quarter. That amount is distributed according to benchmarks we created based on several factors, including seniority, personal skills, attendance, and productivity. Each employee is rated from one to ten (ten being exceptional), which determines their share of the bonus. That means at least $200,000 of our profits every year are going into bonuses.

We have devised a simple formula based on a point system, computed on a spreadsheet. Two people may be doing the exact same job, but one might get a bigger bonus than the other. If they end up comparing notes and one comes to me and asks,

"Why did Joe get more than I did?" I can say, "Well, that's easy. He produces more than you do. If you can show me that that's not true, then I will adjust it." Usually when they check, they find that they have built fewer valves, for example, and they plan to do better in the future!

Will my business survive another generation? I try to stress to my children that they should think not only of our family but of the employees, for whom our company is a source of livelihood. I encourage them to think about our charitable trust, which promotes the Cruz legacy in the Philippines and around the world by providing educations for the next generation of engineers—and the next, and the next.

CONCLUSION

When people think of entrepreneurs these days, they think of exponential growth, of start-up tech companies that scale upward at blinding rates, of college dropouts turned billionaires, of private jets. As a seasoned entrepreneur, I share some genes with today's entrepreneurs, but I know the secrets to staying in power as well. I have shared many of them with you, but here are some more.

Let's be honest—most entrepreneurs are gamblers. I don't mean they go to casinos—though, like me, they might. Most entrepreneurs go into business for themselves knowing that it's a risk. Even though they know it may be a rocky road, they're still willing to take it. They say, "I can improve this industry." So why do so many entrepreneurs fail?

As a seasoned entrepreneur, I share some genes with today's entrepreneurs, but I know the secrets to staying power as well.

To be an entrepreneur you have to ride your failures. You have to meet the risks with persistence. And some people just can't do that. They give up too quickly.

If you want your business to be successful, you need to grow incrementally. If you go overboard and take on too much too quickly, you will most likely fail. We have built Valve Research very, very slowly over the last forty years. It's been a very gentle slope—but it's always been an upward trend.

You could say that the valve industry doesn't have dramatic ups and downs, that it's very steady. But that's because we *made*

183

it that way. I'm a talented salesperson; I could have scaled orders exponentially, but if for some reason we couldn't deliver, we would have fallen like a rock. I could have expanded into additional industries, such as aerospace or satellites, but I knew that spreading ourselves too thinly would not be a good decision in the long term.

We write our own programs to design components. From design to delivery, a valve could take six months—and it could take six years for that valve to become profitable. But once the valve matures, you really start making money. For the company to remain steady, you need to have many different contracts going all the time. You can't be overly dependent on one customer. Fortunately I learned this lesson early in my career at Lucas Rotax in Canada. Their only customer was the Canadian Air Force, and when the Air Force decided not to build the CF-105 anymore, my job (and thousands of others) were gone. The company had to rush to try to get other contracts, but it can take forever to win another contract. They should have been building engines for more than one company in order to balance growth.

Aircraft companies are famous for concentrating on one kind of airplane. At one time there were many airplane builders around the world, but now in the United States we have Boeing and maybe one or two other major companies. Airbus in Europe is big, and there are a few others, but the rest have gone by the wayside. The surviving companies build a lot of planes.

I believe in entrepreneurship, and I believe in engineering. That's why I founded my charitable trust—to get more people interested in engineering and in building a better world. I'm a great believer that every country on the map needs manufacturing jobs. Whether it's airplanes or buildings or software, engineering creates jobs—and it all starts with education.

CONCLUSION

Whether it's airplane, or building, or software, engineering creates jobs—and it all starts with education.

I wrote this book for the young me, for the boy who dreamed about building crystal radio sets that would bring people joy, information, communication—and give them hope. In 88 years I have never lost the belief that ideas can change lives. I've lived long enough to see my ideas improve my own life, my children's and grandchildren's lives, and those of my employees—and now to create a new generation of thinkers. For an airplane to soar it needs its valves to succeed. For this world to improve, it needs *your* idea, no matter how small.

Made in the USA
Columbia, SC
15 July 2024

38367385R00114